THE IMPORTANCE OF BEING EARNEST

A Reader's Companion

TWAYNE'S MASTERWORK STUDIES

Robert Lecker, General Editor

THE IMPORTANCE OF BEING EARNEST

A Reader's Companion

Peter Raby

TWAYNE PUBLISHERS • NEW YORK
Maxwell Macmillan Canada • Toronto
Maxwell Macmillan International • New York Oxford Singapore Sydney

Twayne's Masterwork Series No. 144

The Importance of Being Earnest: A Reader's Companion
Peter Raby

Twayne Publishers   Maxwell Macmillan Canada, Inc.
Macmillan Publishing Co.   1200 Eglinton Avenue
866 Third Avenue   Suite 200
New York, New York 10022   Don Mills, Ontario M3C 3N1

Library of Congress Cataloging-in-Publication Data

Raby, Peter.
    The importance of being earnest : a reader's companion / Peter
Raby.
        p. cm.—(Twayne's masterwork studies ; no. 144)
    Includes bibliographical references (p.) and index.
    ISBN 0-8057-8587-6.—ISBN 0-8057-8588-4 (pbk.)
    1. Wilde, Oscar. 1854–1900. Importance of being earnest.
I. Title. II. Series.
PR5818.I45R33   1995
822'.8—dc20   94-33949
                                                     CIP

The paper used in this publication meets the minimum requirements of American
National Standard for Information Sciences—Permanence of Paper for Printed Library
Materials, ANSI Z3948–1984. ∞™

10 9 8 7 6 5 4 3 2 1 (hc)
10 9 8 7 6 5 4 3 2 1 (pb)

Printed in the United States of America

Contents

Oscar Wilde in 1892
Courtesy of the author

Note on the References and Acknowledgments

This study refers to the three-act version of the play, which was the one produced by George Alexander with Wilde's approval and which formed the basis of the text he prepared for publication in 1899. While the four-act version has much of interest and helps to throw some light on the extremely complex process through which Wilde's text took shape, it is inferior as a stage work, and preeminence must surely be given to the version that Wilde twice approved.

The references in the text to *The Importance of Being Earnest* are to the edition by Russell Jackson (London: Benn, 1980; New York: Norton, 1980), and these are in the form of E together with a page number. I have tried to avoid fussiness and have not referenced every small quotation from the text. It is a short play, and it is relatively easy to find your way about in it.

Other references to Wilde's works are to the *Complete Works of Oscar Wilde* (Glasgow: HarprCollins, 1994), and these are given in the form W followed by a page number.

Chronology

1854	Oscar Fingal O'Flahertie Wills Wilde is born in Dublin on 16 October, the second son of Sir William Wilde, an eye-and-ear specialist, and Jane Francesca Elgee, an Irish patriot and writer who used the pseudonym Speranza.
1864–1871	Attends Portora Royal School, Enniskillen, and in his last year wins the Portora Gold Medal as the best classical scholar.
1867	His younger sister, Isola, dies.
1871–1874	Attends Trinity College, Dublin, and is presented with the Berkeley Gold Medal for Greek.
1874	Wins a scholarship to Magdalen College, Oxford, where he comes under the influence of John Ruskin, the Slade Professor of Art, and Walter Pater.
1875	Travels in Italy.
1876	His father dies.
1877	Wilde travels in Greece and Italy with John Mahaffy, professor of ancient history at Dublin.
1878	Wins Newdigate Prize with his poem "Ravenna" and completes his degree with a double first. Moves to London.
1879–1880	Establishes himself in London society as an exponent of aestheticism. Among his friends are such actresses as the society beauty Lillie Langtry, Helena Modjeska, Sarah Bernhardt, and Ellen Terry, and the painter James Whistler.
1881	Publishes *Poems,* his first book, probably at his own expense. George du Maurier produces a series of cartoons in *Punch,* featuring the poet Maudle and the painter Jellaby Postlethwaite, based on Wilde and Whistler. W. S. Gilbert and Arthur Sullivan collaborate on the light opera *Patience,* a satire

on aestheticism, which D'Oyly Carte presents as the opening production of the Savoy Theatre: the composite aesthetes Bunthorne and Grosvenor are loosely based on Wilde and Whistler, respectively.

1882   Wilde undertakes an extensive lecture tour of the United States and Canada, in conjunction with the New York production of *Patience.* On arrival, is reported to have told a customs officer, "I have nothing to declare except my genius." Lectures on "The English Renaissance," "The House Beautiful," and "The Decorative Arts," drawing many of his ideas from Ruskin and William Morris and, in terms of style, on the writing of Pater and Swinburne. Meets Whitman, Henry James, and Longfellow, and is generally well received by his audiences, though disparaged by most critics.

1883   Spends five months in Paris, where he completes the play *The Duchess of Padua,* commissioned but rejected by the actress Mary Anderson. Briefly visits New York for the production of his first play, *Vera,* withdrawn after a week. On 26 November, becomes engaged to Constance Lloyd, daughter of an Irish lawyer.

1884   Is married in London on 29 May. Spends honeymoon in Paris.

1885   On 1 January moves into 16, Tite Street, Chelsea. Quarrels with Whistler. On 5 June his elder son, Cyril, is born. Wilde writes an increasing number of articles out of need for income. Begins to review books for the *Pall Mall Gazette.*

1886   Meets his close friend and supporter Robert Ross. On 3 November younger son, Vyvyan, is born.

1887–1889   Wilde edits *The Woman's World,* which he transforms.

1888   Publishes a collection of fairy tales, *The Happy Prince and Other Tales.*

1889   Publishes "The Portrait of Mr. W.H.," in which Wilde seeks to identify the "W.H." of the dedication to Shakespeare's sonnets as a boy actor, Willie Hughes, in *Blackwood's Magazine.*

1890   Publishes his novel *The Picture of Dorian Gray* in *Lippincott's Monthly Magazine.* Wilde comments on the characters, "Basil Hallward is what I think I am: Lord Henry what the world thinks me: Dorian is what I would like to be in other ages, perhaps."

1891   Introduced by the poet Lionel Johnson to Lord Alfred Douglas. *The Duchess of Padua* is produced in New York, under the title *Guido Ferranti.* In February, the important essay *The Soul of Man under Socialism* is published in the *Fortnightly Review*. The extended version of *The Picture of Dorian Gray* is published in England, to hostile critical reaction. Wilde publishes a collection of essays, *Intentions,* and two further collections of stories, *Lord Arthur Savile's Crime and Other Stories* and *A House of Pomegranates.* At the end of the year, visits Paris, where he writes *Salomé* in French. Meets Mallarmé, Verlaine, and Proust, and becomes friends with Pierre Louÿs and André Gide.

1892   Wilde's first play to be staged in England, *Lady Windermere's Fan,* opens at the St. James's Theatre on 20 February in a production by George Alexander. Shocks his audience by appearing on stage after the final curtain with a cigarette in his hand and a green carnation in his buttonhole. In June, Sarah Bernhardt begins to rehearse *Salomé* in London, but the Lord Chamberlain refuses to grant a license for public performance because of the play's biblical subject.

1893   *Salomé* published in French. *A Woman of No Importance* is produced at the Theatre Royal, Haymarket, with Sir Herbert Beerbohm Tree as Lord Illingworth and Mrs. Bernard Beere as Mrs. Arbuthnot. In November, *Lady Windermere's Fan* is published.

1894   The English version of *Salomé* is published, with a dedication to Lord Alfred Douglas as the "translator of my play" (Wilde was dissatisfied with the translation, and revised it extensively), and controversial illustrations by Aubrey Beardsley. Wilde also publishes his long poem *The Sphinx* in a limited edition, with a cover designed by Charles Ricketts, and *A Woman of No Importance.* In August, Wilde takes his family to Worthing, where he writes *The Importance of Being Earnest.*

1895   On 3 January, *An Ideal Husband* opens at the Theatre Royal, Haymarket, before an audience that includes the Prince of Wales. During the rehearsals of *The Importance of Being Earnest,* Wilde goes on holiday to North Africa with Douglas, where they meet Gide in Algiers. On 14 February, George Alexander presents *The Importance of Being Earnest* at the St. James's Theatre. The Marquess of Queensberry, Douglas's father, is refused entrance to the theater and leaves a bouquet of vegetables for Wilde at the stagedoor. On 28 February, Wilde finds a card left for him at the Albemarle Club by Queensberry: "To Oscar Wilde posing [as a] Somdomite [sic]." Wilde applies for a warrant for the arrest of Queensberry, for publishing a libel. On 5 April, Queensberry is acquitted. Wilde is arrested, and his first trial for homosexual offenses begins on 26 April. The jury fails to agree. The judge orders a retrial, and on 25 May, Wilde receives a sentence of two years' imprisonment, with hard labor. He is imprisoned first at Pentonville, then Wandsworth, and transferred to Reading on 20 November. He is declared bankrupt. He never sees his children again.

1896   His wife visits Wilde to tell him about the death of his mother, the last meeting between them. *Salomé* is produced (in French) by the avant-garde director A.-M. Lugné-Poe at the Théàtre de l'Oeuvre, Paris, to Wilde's immense gratitude.

1897   Writes a long confessional explanation of his life, one page at a time, in the form of an extended letter to Douglas, eventually published as *De Profundis*. On 19 May, Wilde is released from prison. He crosses the Channel to Dieppe and lives abroad for the rest of his life. For a time, he joins Douglas in Italy.

1898   *The Ballad of Reading Gaol* is published. Wilde's wife, Constance, dies on 7 April.

1899   *The Importance of Being Earnest* and *An Ideal Husband* are published.

1900   After being received into the Roman Catholic church, Wilde dies in the Hôtel d'Alsace, Paris, on 30 November, aged 46.

1905   Robert Ross publishes a much abridged edition of *De Profundis,* omitting all references to Douglas. First English production of *Salomé,* at the Bijou Theatre, London, on 10 May.

1908   *Complete Works of Oscar Wilde* published, edited by Ross.

1909   Wilde's remains are reburied in Père Lachaise cemetery, Paris, with a monument by Epstein.

LITERARY AND
HISTORICAL CONTEXT

1

The Artist as Critic

In "The Decay of Lying," Wilde argued that Life imitated Art far more than Art imitated Life. He used Life, his own life and experience, as material for his Art, in sympathy with Lionel Johnson's declaration that "life must be a ritual." Wilde's elevation of art to the highest end that existence affords responds to the precepts of romanticism as reworked by his Oxford mentor Walter Pater: "To burn always with this hard, gemlike flame, to maintain this ecstasy, is success in life." Wilde's whole life evolved as a conscious process of self-expression and self-dramatization. He saw his role as an artist in terms of a vocation, one that became for him, in the end, impossible to reconcile with social convention. His comment on Tennyson indicates the distance he perceived between the sacred calling of the artist and the daily life of the conventional Victorian family man: "How can a man be a great poet and lead the life of an English country-gentleman? Think of a man going down to breakfast at eight o'clock with the family, and writing *Idylls of the King* until lunchtime."[1]

Wilde's concept of the artist led him to take a relentlessly public and active role, of which his own voice and physical appearance were essential components. During his career he acquired many voices, personas, and masks. Some of the more notable were the salon conversationalist, the storyteller, the connoisseur, and the public lecturer. Like a good actor, he usually showed an instinctive awareness of the nature of his audience, whether in a private or a public context. In much of his writing, too, the notion of the speaking voice is prominent; behind the tales one is conscious of the personality of the storyteller; in the critical dialogues and the drama the form itself acknowledges and exploits the oral medium, and the same acknowledgment exists, in a different way, in the confessional letter that became known as *De Profundis* and in *The Ballad of Reading Gaol.*

Wilde, then, is the archetypal artist of late romanticism, one of the figures not only associated with the doctrines of aestheticism and their hothouse flowering in the decadent 1890s but someone who epitomized them. He was satirized by W. S. Gilbert in *Patience* as Reginald Bunthorne, the fleshly poet: "Though the Philistines may jostle you will rank as an apostle in the high aesthetic band, / If you walk down Piccadilly with a poppy or a lily in your mediaeval hand." By the mid-nineties, the lily had become an orchid in the popular mind. It was reported that, on Wilde's arrest, he was carrying a copy of the *Yellow Book,* an assumption that linked Wilde with Beardsley, the illustrator of *Salomé,* and with the avant-garde in both writing and the illustrative arts. The two most ostensibly decadent works that Wilde completed were a play that was rejected by the censor for performance in England, *Salomé,* and a novel that seemed to hint at corruption, *The Picture of Dorian Gray,* the preface of which defiantly declares, "There is no such thing as a moral or immoral book. Books are well written, or badly written. That is all" (W17).

But while Wilde involved himself with the more rarefied end of the literary spectrum, with books for a specialized readership, books beautifully designed and illustrated, in limited editions, he was also active in the world of journalism, as contributor and editor; and the modernist, symbolist play *Salomé* was preceded and followed by comedies especially conceived for the commercial theater. *Salomé* was eventually performed for the first time while Wilde was in prison, by the leading French experimental director A.-M. Lugné-Poe in Paris, in a sequence of plays that included Henrik Ibsen's *Peer Gynt* and the flagship of surrealist drama, *Ubu Roi,* by Alfred Jarry. Wilde was clearly in touch with continental developments in drama, especially those on the Paris stage, and with the innovations of Ibsen. The genre that he chose to explore and develop was that of society comedy. Wilde's visual sense gave him a keen perception of the importance of setting and costume on the stage. He had a close knowledge of the contemporary commercial theater and was on intimate terms with a number of actresses and actors. His surprising emergence as a writer of polished comedies was built on more experience than might be immediately apparent. His debut was prompted by the actor-manager George Alexander, who assumed the management of the St. James's Theatre in 1890 and asked Wilde for a play. Alexander rejected the offer of Wilde's pastiche revenge drama *The Duchess of Padua,* suggested that Wilde should write on a modern subject, and made him an advance of £50. Wilde took himself off to the Lake District. "I wonder can I do it in a week, or will it take three?" he asked Frank Harris. "It ought not to take long to beat the Pineros and the Joneses."[2]

Lady Windermere's Fan is a remarkable beginning, and certainly more than adequate competition for plays such as Arthur Wing Pinero's *Lady Bountiful* or Henry Arthur Jones's *The Triumph of the Philistines.* Wilde seems to have absorbed, and to reflect, a number of theatrical traditions and yet to have formulated his own distinctive style and method. There are echoes of the situation and style of the English comedy of manners, stretching back through Sheridan to Congreve; there are clear affinities with the social dramas of Dumas *fils* and Sardou, two of the French authors who provided the seemingly inexhaustible supply of plots and motifs on which the English theater drew unashamedly, and with the broader, less subtle genre of melodrama. Wilde was also responsive to the concerns and methods of Ibsen. *A Doll's House* had been given its first London performance in 1889; *Hedda Gabler* and *Ghosts* followed in 1891. Of *Hedda Gabler,* Wilde wrote that he "felt pity and terror, as though the play were Greek." Wilde was a good friend and supporter of the American actress Elizabeth Robins, a leading Ibsen exponent, and maintained his interest in Ibsen's plays, asking from prison for translations of *Little Eyolf* and *John Gabriel Borkman.* In essence, he saw himself as a competitor. His own plays can be seen as "issue" plays and share with Ibsen the attack, both direct and oblique, on the inherited value system of nineteenth-century morality. He chose, however, to work within the system of the managements of fashionable West End theaters, dominated by men such as George Alexander, Herbert Beerbohm Tree, and Charles Wyndham. Elizabeth Robins, patronized and, she felt, exploited, rebelled. Shaw, in his early career as a playwright, initially found it extremely difficult to find an appropriate venue for his Ibsenite, Wildean plays and had recourse to the independent theater movement, with smaller audiences of like-minded people, brief runs, and slender profits. Wilde generously linked Shaw to himself, thanking him, on reception of *Widowers' Houses,* for "Op. 2 of the great Celtic School."[3] (Op. 1 was *Lady Windermere's Fan;* Op. 3, *A Woman of No Importance;* and Op. 5, *An Ideal Husband,* which he was itching to begin.) But in the first half of the nineties, Wilde was really out on his own in reconciling his high artistic aims with the blatantly commercial medium of the London stage.

To comment on the social and historical background to *The Importance of Being Earnest* may seem a slightly redundant and heavy-handed approach to a farcical comedy. But the rise of Wilde as an artist coincided with the closing of a century in which the fundamental beliefs and structures, religious, philosophical, political, social, economic, were increasingly fragile. Ostensibly, England was at the height of its power, with a long-lived queen (whom Wilde admired) at its head who was also empress of India. At home, the country seemed stable, dominated by the wealth and snobbery of a secure aristocracy and upper-middle class; abroad, commerce and the gunboat ensured British prosperity. The European nation-states had presided over the carve-up of Africa in the most blatant example of collective imperialism in modern times, and while large tracts of the world map were being colored red, nearer at hand the colonial occupation of Ireland was becoming an increasingly urgent issue. The unquestioning assumptions of the right of the white man, and especially the British, to rule lie behind the text of Wilde's plays: Lord Illingworth offers Gerald Arbuthnot a post as his secretary in India in *A Woman of No Importance,* the country where Algernon and Ernest's father, General

Moncrieff, served and, presumably, died. The ex-colonies provide a useful source of wealth in the form of Mr. Hopper in *Lady Windermere's Fan.* To be American, like Hester Worsley in *A Woman of No Importance,* is to be, from society's point of view, brash and without style. The society in which Wilde sets his plays is fundamentally male-orientated, God-fearing, white, aristocratic, moneyed.

It is also under pressure, pressure that would contribute to the European unrest that erupted in the First World War, the Russian Revolution, and the Easter Rising and civil war in Ireland, rather than the acts of violence in Grosvenor Square envisaged by Lady Bracknell. Wilde's jokes surreptitiously draw attention to the impermanence, and absurdity, of the prevailing social and political structures and to the inherited complacency that cocoons them. "Really," as Algernon comments in the opening moments of the play, "if the lower orders don't set us a good example, what on earth is the use of them?" "Who was your father?" Lady Bracknell inquires of Jack. "He was evidently a man of some wealth. Was he born in what the Radical papers call the purple of commerce, or did he rise from the ranks of the aristocracy?" Lady Bracknell, the apparent guardian of the status quo, reveals the hollowness beneath the facade of English "Society" by her implication that wealth is even more important than breeding and that the double standard applies as much to social respectability as to morality. One should never speak disrespectfully of Society, as she reminds Algernon: "Only people who can't get into it do that." Wilde, Dublin-born, getting into English society on the strength of his wit and yet never quite a part of it, saw English values from an unusual perspective. His plays chart, subtly but incisively, the forces stirring beneath the social fabric, forces to do with belief in a post-Darwinian age, with the place of women in society, and with capitalism and the rise of the working classes—or the "lower orders," in Algernon's phrase. In the world of *The Importance of Being Earnest,* the servants as well as their masters drink the champagne. The idyll that Wilde created was received by a St. James's audience composed largely of those who ascribed to, and indeed represented, the massive assurance of the late Victorian establishment. But even at the tribal ritual of a fashionable first night, some of them may have sensed the subversion of Wilde's deceptive text.

The plays were launched in London, but Wilde was also conscious of the American market. All three society comedies had New York productions, and his negotiations through his agent, Elisabeth Marbury, especially with the producer Charles Frohman, ensured that he was well rewarded. Frohman's offers, in fact, may have been indirectly responsible for *The Importance of Being Earnest,* for he was pressing Wilde to write a modern *School for Scandal* type of comedy. In turning to farce, Wilde was apparently taking a backward step, at least in the view of Shaw, who complained that "the general effect is that of a farcical comedy dating from the [eighteen] seventies, unplayed during that period because it was too clever and too decent, and brought up to date as far as possible by Mr Wilde in his now completely formed style."[4] Less-subjective critics have judged that Wilde, while embracing the "low" form of farce, perhaps the most public and available of all nineteenth-century genres, triumphantly transformed it into a glittering and unique artifice.

2

The Triumph of the "Trivial"

The Importance of Being Earnest is one of the world's great comedies, yet its writer is one of the British authors whose international appeal might have been thought unlikely. A small part of this interest may spring from Wilde's notoriety and the way in which his glittering, successful life was so swiftly and savagely changed into a particularly public tragedy. He has acquired the status of a cultural icon, so that books or films with his name attached—*Oscar Wilde's London* and *The Trials of Oscar Wilde,* for example—will sell on the connection alone. But that allure does not account for the continuing popularity of his writing, among the best-known of which are works as diverse as *The Ballad of Reading Gaol,* fairy stories such as "The Happy Prince" and "The Selfish Giant," *The Picture of Dorian Gray, Salomé* (though usually transmitted in the operatic version of Richard Strauss), and *The Importance of Being Earnest.* His other comedies rise and fall in critical and popular judgment: since the 1980s, they have been experiencing a strong revival, with subtle and innovative interpretations, such as Philip Prowse's production of *A Woman of No Importance* for the Royal Shakespeare Company. *The Importance of Being Earnest,* ever since it became firmly established by George Alexander's revival of his own original production in 1909, has scarcely wavered in its stage appeal and has become one of the most frequently performed plays in the modern English-language repertory. With highlights such as John Gielgud's productions, the 1952 Anthony Asquith film, and Peter Hall's interpretation for the National Theatre in London in 1982, the play has maintained its effortlessly achieved status as a classic.

Unusually for a play apparently so concerned with minute details of manners set in a specific era and a rarefied milieu, the text is almost indestuctible, though never easy to bring fully to life. Something of Wilde's unique creation always manages to survive. Wilde was self-confessedly and professedly a modern writer. As a dramatist, he was a younger contemporary of Ibsen. As he ended his career as a play-wright, Lugné-Poe was preparing to stage Alfred Jarry's *Ubu Roi*, the forerunner of the surreal and the absurd. Wilde seems instinctively to have anticipated some of the trends that have emerged more fully in the drama of the second half of the twentieth century. Certainly his plays, and above all his last comedy, take on a new dimension when viewed from a post-Beckett, post-Ionesco, post-Stoppard perspective. His play is a landmark in the theater and one whose reputation is growing rather than receding.

Precisely why this should be so is harder to pin down. Contemporary critics, who were generally favorable, thought that Wilde had constructed something with a rather limited shelf life. A few other comedies and farces survive from the 1890s: Brandon Thomas's *Charley's Aunt,* for example, retains its fun, but remains a period piece. Pinero's work is interesting, often revealing, but unmistakably late Victorian. Even Shaw's best comedies, like *Arms and the Man,* do not convey that ultimate freedom from context and that sense of authority and autonomy that is the hallmark of *The Importance of Being Earnest.*

Lewis Carroll's *Alice's Adventures in Wonderland,* together with its sequel, *Through the Looking Glass,* is an earlier Victorian work, though in a different genre, that achieves a comparable freedom. In a television interview about Eugene Ionesco and the theater of the absurd, the British director Jonathan Miller suggested that the English did not need a specific theater of the absurd because that vein of surreal, anarchic humor was already present in their literature. There are several analogies between Carroll's fantastic dream landscape and the luminous stage world of *The Importance of Being Earnest*. Both play with the polite conventions and restrictions of Victorian society. Both evoke the appearance of childlike innocence, a facade that rapidly crumbles once the narrative picks up speed. Both hint at the scarcely mentionable desires and appetites that surge beneath the thin veneer of manners and custom. Each is energetically subversive, and in a way that seems infinitely transferable to a wide range of situations and societies.

Although *The Importance of Being Earnest* has long been recognized as a theatrical masterpiece, literary critics have, perhaps understandably, been slightly wary of writing too much about it. Comedies are notoriously difficult to analyze, and a farcical comedy that degree more dangerous. Wilde overlapped with Ibsen and Shaw; but many of the early English productions of Ibsen, and indeed the first phase of Shaw's work for the stage, were in small, experimental theaters, promoted by enthusiasts and societies. Wilde was one of the first serious writers—that is, a writer who took himself seriously as an artist—to use the modern English commercial theater as his medium. Plays in the commercial theater of the 1890s were regarded primarily as entertainments, not vehicles for the most fastidious of stylists. It was more than half a century before critics and commentators were prepared to take "seriously" a self-proclaimed "trivial" play. Wilde's personal tragedy was partly responsible for this neglect, coupled with the additional difficulty of writing about a work designed to be seen and heard rather than read. But Wilde has benefited from the relatively recent upsurge of interest in performance art as a whole and from the even more recent focus on film, television, fashion, and other less literary and elitist forms.

Interest in Wilde, in his plays, and in *The Importance of Being Earnest* as his masterpiece has risen steadily through the twentieth century. A number of critical studies have given greater emphasis to Wilde's dramatic writing, recognizing it as modern, experimental and still partly unexplored in theatrical terms. Richard Ellmann's great biography laid out Wilde's personal and artistic complexity with lucid objectivity and sympathy. Recent studies of Western culture have given Wilde new prominence, as in Camille Paglia's *Sexual Personae,* which has two long chapters on Wilde, including one entitled "The English Epicene: Wilde's *The Importance of Being Earnest.*" Wilde's work is more and more seen as a substantial and unusual achievement, with *The Importance of Being Earnest* as a key text rather than simply a brilliant but essentially irrelevant accident.

Each reader provides a new interpretation, but each production recreates and reinvents a dramatic text in a collaborative and specific way. *The Importance of Being Earnest,* by its very nature as a particular kind of "trivial comedy," carries an aura of exclusiveness and elusiveness. Wilde warned his critics, "For the criticism of such a complex mode of art as the drama the highest culture is necessary. No one can criticise drama who is not capable of receiving impressions from the other arts also." He issued a challenge to his audience and his readers that, even after a hundred years, has perhaps not yet been fully answered.

3

Taking Wilde Seriously

Most of the critics who attended the first night of *The Importance of Being Earnest*—they occupied between 70 and 100 seats at St. James's Theatre openings—were reviewing their second new Wilde play in six weeks. *An Ideal Husband* had opened at the Theatre Royal, Haymarket, on 3 January and was still running. This fact drew attention to the contrast in style and form between the two plays, and many of the notices attempted to define the precise nature of Wilde's newest work. The placing of plays in precise categories was a well-established nineteenth-century practice: like Polonius, pedantic critics and theater managers went way beyond the simple categories of tragedy and comedy to identify poetic drama, melodrama and all its variations (domestic, nautical, historical, etc.), drama (after the French *drame*), burlesque, and farce. Then there was recognition of changes in dramatic technique, such as the "cup-and-saucer" dramas of Tom Robertson, with their detailed realism, and the "problem play" and the "New Drama," heralded in particular by Ibsen. Wilde characteristically played the label game, identifying both *A Woman of No Importance* and *An Ideal Husband* as "a new and original play of modern life" and having the description "A Trivial Comedy for

Serious People" printed on the programs of *The Importance of Being Earnest*. He expanded this challenge in an interview that appeared in *Black and White* on 16 February 1895. There he described his newest play as "exquisitely trivial, a delicate bubble of fancy" and praised the first act as ingenious, the second as beautiful, and the third as abominably clever. *The Importance of Being Earnest* was called "a pure farce of Gilbertian parentage" *(New York Times); a* "farcical comedy dating from the seventies" (by a rather grumpy George Bernard Shaw in the *Saturday Review*); "a bid for popularity in the direction of farce" *(Theatre); and* "really artistic burlesque" (H. G. Wells in the *Pall Mall Gazette*). In addition to defining the category of a play, reviewers tended to trace its pedigree, a trait more understandable when so much commercial drama was unashamedly derivative. The influences and precursors cited most frequently were W. S. Gilbert, A. W. Pinero, the farce writer H. J. Byron, and, from earlier times, Marivaux and Sheridan.

Two of the most perceptive reviews were by William Archer in the *World* (20 February 1895) and by A. B. Walkley in the *Spectator* (23 February 1895). Archer—arguably, with Shaw, the foremost English theater critic of the day—was the champion and translator of Ibsen. He supported the idea of an endowed theater and had published an influential book of essays in 1886, *About the Theatre*. Archer recognized *The Importance of Being Earnest* as, above all, a play that it was good to see but was essentially elusive. He referred to Pater's comment on the tendency of all art to verge toward the absolute art of music, anticipating W. H. Auden's later description of the play as the "only pure verbal opera in English."[1] Archer wrote, "He [Pater] might have found an example in *The Importance of Being Earnest,* which imitates nothing, represents nothing, means nothing, is nothing, except a sort of *rondo capriccioso,* in which the artist's fingers run with crisp irresponsibility up and down the keyboard of life. Why attempt to analyse and class such a play? Its theme, in other hands, would have made a capital farce; but 'farce' is far too gross and commonplace a word to apply to such an iridescent filament of fantasy." Archer also praised Wilde's theatrical instinct:

In all his plays, and certainly not least in this one, the story is excellently told and illustrated with abundance of scenic detail. Monsieur Sarcey himself (if Mr. Wilde will forgive my saying so) would "chortle in his joy" over John Worthing's entrance in deep mourning (even down to his cane) to announce the death of his brother Ernest, when we know that Ernest in the flesh—a false but undeniable Ernest—is at that moment in the house making love to Cecily. The audience does not instantly awaken to the meaning of his inky suit, but even as he marches solemnly down the stage, and before a word is spoken, you can feel the idea kindling from row to row, until a "sudden glory" of laughter fills the theatre. It is only the born playwright who can imagine and work up to such an effect.

Wilde's mastery of the visual dimension of theater is part of his legacy to future dramatists such as Stoppard and Ayckbourn.

A. B. Walkley went a little further than Archer, declaring "with no ironic intention" that Wilde had found himself, at last, as an "artist in sheer nonsense." He wrote, "In his farce at the St. James's—Mr. Archer, I see, thinks the word 'farce' derogatory here; but why? We call *The Wasps* and *Le Médecin malgré Lui* farces—in his farce, then, *The Importance of Being Earnest,* there is no discordant note of seriousness. It is of nonsense all compact, and better nonsense, I think, our stage has not seen." Walkley then proceeded to survey the development of, and attitudes toward, comedy, from Aristotle onward, dwelling on the ferociously cruel fun of Molière and then defining the "abandonment of realism for fantasy" that he saw in the work of Pinero and Gilbert. However, he argued, enough of realism (or, at any rate, of oblique reference to life) remained in their farces to mingle a little contempt with the laughter. "Now the merit of *The Importance of Being Earnest* is that the laughter it excites is absolutely free from bitter afterthought. Mr. Wilde makes his personages ridiculous, but—you will admit the distinction?—he does not ridicule them. He introduces personages ostensibly of to-day, young men 'about town,' 'revolting' daughters, a clergyman, a prim governess, a glib valet; but he does not poke fun at them as types; he induces us to laugh at their conduct for its sheer whimsicality, not as illustrating the foibles of their class." Walkley went on to give an extraordinarily sharp explanation of the reason for the laughter Wilde's play evoked, based on a then-current belief that the necessary condition for laughter is the simultaneous recognition of the absurd and the natural in the thing laughed at. He used as his example the arrival of Jack in mourning clothes: "The mere sight of him in this garb sets us off laughing. For we guess at once what he is going to do; and we have just seen his bosom friend arrive at the house in the assumed character of the very Ernest who is now to be given out as dead. Why do we laugh? Because, knowing what we do, we recognise John's conduct as absurd; but, on the other hand, we recognise it, given only his knowledge, as natural. So with all the actions of the play." The cumulative result is that you "have something like real life in detail, yet, in sum, absolutely unlike it; the familiar materials of life shaken up, as it were, and rearranged in a strange, unreal pattern." In sum, "you are in a world that is real yet fantastic; . . . you have fallen among amiable, gay, and witty lunatics."

The unusual qualities of Wilde's comedy that Walkley and Archer responded to were also noted by the reviewer in *Truth*,[2] who thought that the chief reason why the piece was so amusing was because it was so completely dominated by its author. There was no attempt at characterization: "All the *dramatis personae,* from the heroes down to their butlers, talk pure and undiluted Wildese." Ironically, but perhaps predictably, the one critic of note who did not respond to this new, pure Wildean comedy of the absurd was Shaw, who found the humor inhuman and "adulterated by stock mechanical fun to an extent that absolutely scandalizes one in a play with such an author's name to it." Shaw wished to be touched by comedy, to be moved to laughter. His own comedies had serious purposes. In a letter printed in Frank Harris's biography of Wilde in 1916, Shaw went further, categorizing the play as "essentially hateful" and heartless.[3] Shaw's coolness offended Wilde, who had hailed him as part of a grand Irish alliance of two against the English literary and critical establishment. He forgave him sufficiently to send him a copy of the published text in 1899. Shaw used the idea of the separated family being reunited, a "stock mechanical" convention if ever there was one and one that Wilde handles so lightly, in his own attempt at farce, *You Never Can Tell,* begun a few months later. Writing retrospectively to Harley Granville-Barker, Shaw underlined the link with his own play's prototype: "It has always seemed merely a farce written round a waiter. It ought to be a very serious comedy, dancing gaily to a happy ending round the grim earnest of Mrs. Clandon's marriage & her XIXth century George-Eliotism."[4]

One other contemporary critic who sensed the level and nature of Wilde's achievement was his friend Max Beerbohm (remembered by Wilde as "Maxbohm" in the list of generals with ghastly names in Act Three). Reviewing the 1902 revival in the *Saturday Review,* he recognized that the play was unlike any other: "In its kind it still seems perfect." The characters "speak a kind of beautiful nonsense—the language of high comedy, twisted into fantasy. Throughout the dialogue is the horse-play of a distinguished intellect and a distinguished imagination—a horse-play among words and ideas, conducted with poetic dignity."[5] The 1902 revival by George Alexander had only limited commercial success, and it was not until Alexander brought it back for an extended run in 1909 that *The Importance of Being Earnest* became firmly established as a key work within the modern English repertory.

The year before, 1908, saw the publication of the complete works and the complete plays, by Methuen, edited by Robert Ross, which provided the context for a perceptive review by St. John Hankin. He, too, recognized the special nature of *The Importance of Being Earnest,* calling it "the nearest approach to absolute originality that he attained" and "the most serious work that Wilde produced for the theatre." Not only is it by far the most brilliant of his plays considered as literature, but it is also the most sincere. "With all its absurdity, its psychology is truer, its criticism of life subtler and more profound, than that of the other plays." Hankin also praises Wilde's technique, somewhat paradoxically, for being more "naturalistic" and comes up with a new definition for its form, "psychological farce, the farce of ideas", a category that he credits Wilde with inventing and among whose successors he numbers Shaw's *Arms and the Man* and *The Philanderer*.[6]

The question of "naturalism," the extent to which the play is seen as about people or about ideas, about surface or about "heart," hovers around responses to *The Importance of Being Earnest* and is clearly crucial in deciding how to direct and to act it. Mary McCarthy, curiously for so brilliant a critic, lined up with Shaw as a strong dissentient voice in objecting to the play's coldness, in a review reprinted in *Sights and Spectacles:* "Clever as it was, it was his first really heartless play. In the others the chivalry of the eighteenth-century Irishman and the romance of the disciple of Théophile Gautier (Oscar was really old-fashioned in the Irish way, except as a critic of morals) not only gave a certain kindness and gallantry to the serious passages and to the handling of women, but provided that proximity of emotion without which laughter, however irresistible, is destructive and sinister. In *The Importance of Being Earnest* this had vanished; and the play, though extremely funny, was essentially hateful."[7]

Mary McCarthy's piece on *The Importance of Being Earnest* started life as a review and is representative of one major trend in Wilde criticism, the evaluation, and revaluation, of individual works. This has always existed alongside the more sensational, Wilde-centered set of reactions, which tended to dwell on the circumstances of Wilde's private life, as exposed by the trials. *The Importance of Being Earnest* won recognition earlier than the rest of Wilde's writing, but as the twentieth century progressed it was joined by Wilde's other plays (even, after Berkoff's successful production, by *Salomé*) to form a body of work substantial enough to warrant critical reappraisal. Studies such as Katharine Worth's *Oscar Wilde* (1983) in the Macmillan Modern Dramatists Series served to emphasize Wilde's centrality as a post-Ibsen modernist and as a precursor for a number of trends in twentieth-century drama and theater. Other writers explored the particular achievements of Wilde as a dramatist, including Joseph Donohue in his grand scheme to reconstruct the performance text of *The Importance of Being Earnest*.[8] The notion that Wilde wrote his plays rapidly and carelessly, a view to which he characteristically contributed, does not bear scrutiny; detailed examination and commentary on individual texts by Ian Small and Russell Jackson have helped to dispell the myth. Much recent Wilde criticism has centered on the complexity of Wilde's dramatic writing and on performance values revealed by studying both past and recent productions.

One major study is Kerry Powell's *Oscar Wilde and the Theatre of the 1890s* (1990). Powell sets Wilde very clearly in the context of the contemporary English theater and shows how he both absorbed and reflected in his plays the ideas and theatrical innovations of Ibsen. He also analyzes a wide range of contemporary English dramatic writing, both the familiar and, more startlingly, the almost forgotten and unpublished, by trawling through the play scripts in the lord chamberlain's files in the British Museum. He establishes how attuned Wilde's plays were to the themes, motifs, and stage language of the 1890s theater. In two key chapters, he traces the parallels between *The Importance of Being Earnest* and a farce at Terry's Theatre, *The Foundling,* and then proceeds to draw attention to "Algernon's other brothers": "On the one hand unique, 'a genre in itself,' on the other *The Importance of Being Earnest* is a shameless ingathering of devices which characterized Victorian farce." In his conclusion, Powell argues that Wilde adapted "not a particular play, but an entire genre—practically cataloguing its varied devices, yet somehow creating a fresh impression rather than only collocating what others had done before him."[9]

The sense of the performance dimension is also dominant in the 1994 study by Joel Kaplan and Sheila Stowell, *Theatre and Fashion: Oscar Wilde to the Suffragettes,* which explores the shifting relationship between theater, fashion, and society in the period between *Lady Windermere's Fan* and the Great War. The study begins with a dazzling analysis of the coded messages carried by the women's dresses and appearances in Wilde's three social comedies, paving the way for a possible examination of this element in *The Importance of Being Earnest,* which is not in fact discussed. The aspect of Wilde as a conscious manipulator of his audience and readers, of his public, has been lucidly expressed by Regenia Gagnier in *The Idylls of the Marketplace* (1986).

In terms of Wilde studies in general, the arrival of Richard Ellmann's major biography was clearly a landmark. It put Wilde on the map for a new generation of readers, even if some of its details are speculative and in spite of its underlying construction of Wilde's life and career in the form of tragedy. Two other broad approaches to Wilde have been apparent. The first is to address Wilde's homosexuality and to see it as something positive that assisted his writing and helped to shape and color individual works, including *The Importance of Being Earnest*. This aspect of Wilde has been given emphasis in studies such as Jonathan Dollimore's *Sexual Dissidence: Augustine to Wilde, Freud to Foucault* (1991), Richard Dellamora's *Masculine Desire: The Sexual Politics of Victorian Aestheticism* (1990), and Elaine Showalter's *Sexual Anarchy: Gender and Culture at the Fin de Siècle* (1991). An alternative view, more in tune with the main thrust of the theater historians, is laid out by Ian Small in *Oscar Wilde Revalued: An Essay on New Materials and Methods of Research* (1993), which, in reaction against Ellmann's tragic dimension, sees Wilde as an industrious writer as well as an artist: a journalist, reviewer, editor, and, above all, a detached and wholly professional dramatist, "a professional writer engaged with all aspects of the marketing and production of his plays."[10]

Critics who have gone back to Wilde's plays in the light of recent developments in the theater have been able to see Wilde's apparent detachment as a positive quality. The different kind of theater language explored by playwrights such as Beckett, Ionesco, Albee, and Stoppard have created a context in which the brittle elegance of Wilde's language, his sense of symmetry, his mastery of pace and pause, his acute visual awareness have been released from the tradition of character and emotion. Katherine Worth, for example, one of the best critics to have examined Wilde's plays from a thoroughly informed theatrical perspective, saw *The Importance of Being Earnest* as "a philosophical farce, an existential farce, to use the modern term which modern criticism is beginning to see as appropriate for this witty exploration of identities."[11] (At the play's culmination, after all, is Jack's question "Lady Bracknell, I hate to seem inquisitive, but would you kindly inform me who I am?") Wilde may have looked back toward Gautier, but in this last play he was instinctively anticipating a new kind of drama, just as his young contemporary Alfred Jarry was in Paris with his iconoclastic *Ubu Roi*. David Parker, in "Oscar Wilde's Great Farce," analyzed the "sense of absurdity behind order, central to Wilde's vision," which, he argued, the play in its entirety demonstrates: "To the contemplation of Nothingness, of the absurd, Wilde brings qualities of wit, intelligence and (not least) appetite for life, rarely found so abundantly in such a context. *The Importance of Being Earnest* is a great farce because it transcends the normal limitations of the form."[12]

There is justice in Wilde's vast claim, in *De Profundis,* that "I took the drama, the most objective form known to art, and made it as personal a mode of expression as the lyric or the sonnet, at the same time that I widened its range and enriched its characterisation." Eric Bentley, in his account of *The Importance of Being Earnest* in *The Playwright as Thinker,* reminded us of Wilde's absorption in the idea of the mask and quoted him: "A Truth in Art is that whose contradictory is also true. The Truths of metaphysics are the Truths of masks." Bentley added, "These words lead us to Pirandello."[13] Bentley's insight draws our attention to the strong sense of role, of archetype, that pervades the play. The "characters" are, to some exent, travesties: each individual inhabits a conventional role, such as the "serious lover" or the "blocking parent," but at the same time subverts it and, in places, transforms it. This aspect of the play was well expressed by Richard Foster in his essay "Wilde as Parodist: A Second Look at *The Importance of Being Earnest*": "The characters know they are in a play, and they know what kind of play it is. Cecily and Gwendolen 'do' parodies of themselves as they assist their lovers in their own self-ridiculing transformation from cynical wits to true men of feeling. The same is true of Prism and Chasuble, even of Lane, who knows perfectly well that he is the type of the wry butler-confidant who is smarter than his employer."[14]

Time has altered our perceptions of farce and of comedy. Unlike the late nineteenth century, with its genially condescending dismissal of farce to the margins, the present sees the genre, especially in the hands of a great artist, as central. In Joseph Bristow's 1992 edition,

The Importance of Being Earnest and Related Writings, he places the play alongside "The Critic as Artist," "The Soul of Man under Socialism," "A Few Maxims for the Instruction of the Over-Educated," and "Phrases and Philosophies for the Use of the Young," thereby integrating it within the main body of Wilde's work. His introduction argues that Wilde's flamboyant writing challenged conventional distinctions. "The point is, in this ethos of rhetorical one-upmanship, there is no pretence to realism. Plot and language have full rein instead. Wilde's comedy marks a radical departure from earlier forms of drama. In fact, in *Earnest*—where everything is exceptionally artificial—there are the beginnings of a theatre of 'alienation' or 'estrangement,' which would become a cornerstone of European modernism, especially in the dramas of Bertolt Brecht. *Earnest,* as its first reviewers noted, has the effect of distancing the audience from its furious turns of phrase."[15]

That sense of distance emerges as one of the perceived strengths of *The Importance of Being Earnest,* a quality that Wilde aimed for throughout his career as an artist. The genre of farcical comedy offered him a certain discipline of structure and convention, into which he injected a precision of language he had perfected in other narrative forms. Camille Paglia treats the play as the highpoint in Wilde's work, arguing that it is "a ritual purification" of the earlier *The Picture of Dorian Gray* and *Salomé* and commenting that in it "the failed poet created a magnificent new poetry, one that even he did not recognize."[16] Her challenging analysis is one of a number of recent studies that give Wilde and his last, unique play a central and powerful voice.

A READING

4

The Genesis of the Play

The Importance of Being Earnest represented a conscious attempt by Wilde to experiment with a different kind of play. Between 1891 and 1894, he had written within two distinct genres. He had achieved success in what might be termed "social comedy," plays of modern society and high society that appeared to revolve around a problem or issue, such as the "woman with a past." *Lady Windermere's Fan* (1892) and *A Woman of No Importance* (1893) had brought him a new reputation and considerable financial success, and *An Ideal Husband,* though subject to negotiation and revision, had been effectively completed. He had also written the poetic, symbolist play *Salomé,* too advanced for its day and too controversial to be licensed for performance in England, although the technical reason given was its biblical subject. By 1894, Wilde was under intense pressure in his personal life. He was torn between the needs of his immediate family and of his private self: he had a wife and two young children to support and was also giving financial help to his mother; and he was becoming more and more embroiled in barely clandestine homosexual encounters, dominated by his relationship with Lord Alfred Douglas. Largely as a result of these demands, intensified by his habitual extravagance, he was extremely short of money. His reputation in the theater was riding high, and understandably he saw it as a potential financial lifeline.

For someone in such turmoil, Wilde's output during 1894 was astonishing. He revised *An Ideal Husband,* wrote the contrasting *A Florentine Tragedy* and most of *La Sainte Courtisane,* and finally embarked on an entirely new genre in *The Importance of Being Earnest.* He was in correspondence with a considerable number of producers and managers during the course of the year: with the English actor-managers John Hare and Lewis Waller over *An Ideal Husband;* with Charles Frohman and Albert Palmer in New York in connection with several projects, both existing and unwritten; and with Dion Boucicault, who was producing *Lady Windermere's Fan* in Australia. Frohman, who controlled the American rights to *Lady Windermere's Fan,* was negotiating for *An Ideal Husband.* The year before, he had invited Wilde to write him a new play, perhaps a "modern 'School for Scandal' style of play"; Wilde's American agent, the "brilliant delightful" Elizabeth Marbury, wrote to Wilde in July from Paris with details of Frohman's latest offer, which included an option on his next modern comedy. Albert Palmer was also angling for a new comedy "with no real serious interest."[1]

Completed plays and royalties from productions were no longer enough to keep Wilde's finances buoyant. He turned his extraordinary gift for storytelling to advantage in the form of the scenario. George Alexander, the generous and approachable actor-manager who leased the St. James's Theatre, had produced Wilde's first great theatrical success, *Lady Windermere's Fan.* He expressed an interest in the new comedy Wilde was talking about, and Wilde sent him a detailed plot outline some time in July 1894, explaining that the "the real charm of the play, if it is to have charm, must be in the dialogue." After an extremely detailed account of the "slight" but "adequate" plot, he added, "Well, I think an amusing thing with lots of fun and wit might be made. If you think so, too, and care to have the refusal of it—do let me know—and send me £150. If, when the play is finished, you think it too slight—not serious enough—of course you have the £150 back—I want to go away and write it—and it could be ready in October—as I have nothing else to do—and Palmer is anxious to have a play from me for the States 'with no real serious interest'—just a comedy."

In the three-act scenario Wilde sent, which is clearly the nucleus of *The Importance of Being Earnest,* the two young men are named Lord Alfred Rufford and his great friend from the country, Bertram Ashton. The setting of Act One is an evening party at Lord Alfred Rufford's rooms in Mayfair. Ashton tells Rufford that he has "a ward, etc. very young and pretty. That in the country he has to be serious, etc. that he comes to town to enjoy himself, and has invented a fictitious younger brother of the name of George—to whom all his misdeeds are put down. Rufford is deeply interested about the ward." During the evening, the "guardian" Ashton proposes to Rufford's sister, Lady Maud Rufford, who knows him only as George. They are interrupted by her mother, the Duchess of Selby. Lord Alfred has been suddenly called away to the country and arrives at the guardian's pretty cottage in Act Two as Mr. George Ashton. The story unfolds, though without the "death" of George and with the additional complications of the arrest of Lord Alfred for debts incurred in London by George and matrimonial designs on the guardian from Miss Prism. The handbag business has not yet been invented. Wilde simply writes, "Miss Prism, who had in early days been governess to the Duchess, sets it all right, without intending to do so—everything ends happily." Perhaps the most revealing sentences refer to the antipastoral, fin de siècle values that inhabit the play. The upright guardian is reproached by Lady Maud for his respectable life in the country: he is a justice of the peace, a churchwarden, a philanthropist, and, worse still, a good example. In defense, he appeals to his life in London. She is mollified on condition that he never live in the country: "The country is demoralising: it makes you respectable." In lines that have not survived in the final draft, Lady Maud praises the urban ideal of the nineties: "The simple fare at the Savoy: the quiet life in Piccadilly: the solitude of Mayfair is what you need, etc." "Result," concluded Wilde, carried away by his creation, "Result. Author called. Cigarette called. Manager called. Royalties for a year for author. Manager credited with writing the play. He consoles himself for the slander with bags of red gold. Fireworks."[2]

Early in August, Wilde traveled down to Worthing (a seaside resort in Sussex, as Jack informs Lady Bracknell) with his family, perhaps with the help, or at least the expectation, of Alexander's £150. The day before he left he wrote to Douglas, "I hope to send you the cigarettes, if Simmonds will let me have them. He has applied for his bill. I am overdrawn £41 at the bank: it really is intolerable the want of money. I have not a penny. I can't stand it any longer, but don't know what to do."[3] During August and September, when he was staying at 5, The Esplanade, Worthing, he wrote the first version of the play. The typescript acts that survive from this phase were stamped by Mrs. Marshall's typewriting agency on 19 September. Douglas provided a major distraction, coming down twice while the whole family was there and then descending on Wilde while he was trying to finish the play by himself. "Bored with Worthing, and still more, I have no doubt, with my fruitless efforts to concentrate my attention on my play, the only thing that really interested me at the moment, you insist on being taken to the Grand Hotel at Brighton. The night we arrive you fall ill with that dreadful low fever that is foolishly called the influenza" (W991). The catalogue of recriminations, recalled by Wilde in prison and recorded in *De Profundis,* poured out.

Wilde had the concentration to produce great work in the midst of chaotic personal circumstances. Although he had never written a farcical comedy before, he had the ability to absorb, subsume, and finally subvert the existing tradition of stage farce. Whether Wilde had actually seen many examples is beside the point, although he was a regular and critical theatergoer. He had an instinctive feel for, and knowledge of, popular entertainment, for narrative forms such as the Gothic story, melodrama, the parable. The nineteenth-century theatrical inheritance was rich and diverse, with burlesque, travesty, parody, and farce surrounding the central core of serious drama. A. W. Pinero, who was steeped in the professional theater, had already explored the genre of farce in *The Magistrate* (1885). First-night critics competed with each other to locate sources for *The Importance of Being Earnest,* and several cited W. S. Gilbert's 1877 farce *Engaged.* There are several common incidents and motifs, notably Belinda Treherne stuffing herself with jam tarts, a compulsive or repetitive eating joke also featured in *The Magistrate*. However, the most striking parallel in *Engaged* is the entry of Symperson in deep black, prematurely in mourning for a nephew who has announced that he intends to kill himself:

> *Enter* SYMPERSON *in deep black; he walks pensively, with a white handkerchief to his mouth.*
>
> CHEVIOT HILL: What's the matter?
>
> SYMPERSON: Hallo! You're still alive?
>
> CHEVIOT HILL: Alive? Yes; why *(noticing his dress)*, is anything wrong?
>
> SYMPERSON: No, no, my dear young friend, these clothes are symbolical; they represent my state of mind. After your terrible threat, which I cannot doubt you intend to put at once into execution—
>
> CHEVIOT HILL: My dear uncle, this is very touching; this unmans me. But, cheer up, dear old friend, I have good news for you.
>
> SYMPERSON: *(alarmed)* Good news? What do you mean?
>
> CHEVIOT HILL: I am about to remove the weight of sorrow which hangs so heavily at your heart. Resume your fancy check trousers—I have consented to live.

It may be that the critics' familiarity with this visual joke, the man in mourning for someone the audience knows is still alive, triggered the cross-reference when George Alexander entered as Jack in deep mourning for his fictional younger brother, Ernest, black-edged handkerchief to his mouth, shortly after the arrival of Algy as Ernest (wearing, as it happened, fancy check trousers). There is little verbal resemblance between the plays, as the above extract demonstrates. But one of Wilde's most characteristic traits as a writer was to suggest the familiar, even the formulaic, before shifting the ground of his subtle reworking and re-creating.

Kerry Powell, in his key book *Oscar Wilde and the Theatre of the 1890s,* explored in convincing detail the areas where Wilde draws upon the genre of contemporary farce, with examples such as the obsession with travel, the idea of escape into childhood or to the country, the preoccupation with family relations announced by the very titles themselves, (e.g., *Charley's Aunt, Cousin Jack*). *Godpapa,* Powell comments, even has a character called Bunbury who is subject to an imaginary ailment, and a young girl with an imaginary brother called Ernest.[4] Bunbury, to cement the coincidence, was played by Charles Brookfield, who had lampooned Wilde in his travesty *The Poet and the Puppets* and was to appear as Phipps, the butler, in *An Ideal Husband.* More immediate, in terms of the composition of *The Importance of Being Earnest,* was E. M. Robson and William Lestocq's farce *The Foundling,* which opened at Terry's Theatre in London on 30 August 1894. This play, like Wilde's, has a foundling hero who has lost his parents, not in Worthing but in the seaside resort of Margate. Wilde, as Powell suggested, might have seen the play on a visit to London, though he could also have gleaned plot details from the newspaper reviews. He also had an opportunity to see the piece when it played briefly in Brighton, the seaside town near Worthing that also happened to be the setting for *The Foundling,* on 20 September.

Another strand of material and motif that Wilde drew upon came from the older English comedy of manners. The suave and sophisticated language of Congreve's Restoration comedy and Sheridan's late eighteenth-century comedy offers the closest parallels to Wilde's tone and texture within English drama, and the staging and structure also provide analogies. In early drafts of *Lady Windermere's Fan,* Wilde incorporated his own echo of the screen scene from Sheridan's *The School for Scandal,* later changed to a curtain, and the screen business resurfaced in the four-act version of *The Importance of Being Earnest,* where Algernon and Cecily conceal themselves behind a screen when Lady Bracknell is announced. Lydia Languish in Sheridan's *The Rivals* writes romantic letters to herself, like Cecily.

Another motif of Restoration comedy occurs in Act One of the four-act version, where Algernon is informed that several tradesmen—his wine merchant, his tailor—have called, which echoes the opening sequence of George Etherege's *The Man of Mode,* in which Dorimant may be seen as one of Algernon's precursors. The double life, the fortune seeking, and heiress hunting in the country have long-established antecedents. But as Wilde's play developed, these parallels, echoes, and analogies became less obtrusive, subsumed beneath the texture of the original work of art that he was fashioning.

The richest source for the new play lay within Wilde's own work. The concept of the dandy was one he had explored in all three of his previous comedies, through the roles of Lord Darlington, Mrs. Erlynne, and, in a minor key, Cecil Graham in *Lady Windermere's Fan* and through the darker portraits of Lord Illingworth and Mrs. Allonby in *A Woman of No Importance,* which also includes the cameo of Lord Alfred Rufford, a character almost wholly defined by his gold-tipped cigarettes and his debts:

> LORD ALFRED: They are awfully expensive. I can only afford them when I'm in debt.
>
> LADY STUTFIELD: It must be terribly, terribly distressing to be in debt.
>
> LORD ALFRED: One must have some occupation nowadays. If I hadn't my debts I shouldn't have anything to think about. (W473)

The joke about a man's occupation would be reworked in *The Importance of Being Earnest* and given to Lady Bracknell. There are other premonitions within *A Woman of No Importance,* besides the title, such as the air of leisure that unfolds in the garden setting of the first act, under the yew tree that reappears at the Manor House, Woolton, and the benevolent tyranny and erratic memory of Lady Hunstanton, a prototype of Lady Bracknell. But the play that seems most clearly to contain the germ of *The Importance of Being Earnest* is its immediate predecessor, *An Ideal Husband.*

Here Wilde developed his idea of the dandy in Lord Goring and, in the text prepared for publication, provided additional material in his detailed description: "Thirty-four, but always says he is younger. A well-bred, expressionless face. He is clever, but would not like to be thought so. A flawless dandy, he would be annoyed if he were considered romantic. He plays with life, and is on perfectly good terms with the world. He is fond of being misunderstood. It gives him a post of vantage" (W521). The outline is full of "buts" and qualifications, giving Lord Goring a complexity that is not nearly so marked in, for example, the saturnine and callous Lord Illingworth, whose icy mask rarely slips. Lord Goring is a benevolent dandy, at such ease with the world that he does not need to wound in order to establish his superiority. Uniquely among Wilde's younger characters, he is shown with his father, a relationship that is portrayed as both humorous and affectionate. He stands at the apex of the play's hierarchy of wit and functions not only as Wildean commentator and observer but also as philosopher and judge. Wilde is so taken with this character that he provides another commentary about him in Act Three and equips him with clothes and accessories—silk hat, Inverness cape, white gloves, Louis Seize cane—that are modeled on his own. "His are all the delicate fopperies of Fashion. One sees that he stands in immediate relation to modern life, makes it indeed, and so masters it. He is the first well-dressed philosopher in the history of thought" (W553). Lord Goring, in fact, is by far the most interesting character within the play. He manipulates events and expresses his superiority by his decision to distance himself from the world of public affairs. He is matched by an apparently frivolous, witty, and unsentimental heroine, Mabel Chiltern, a female dandy who anticipates Gwendolen and Cecily just as Lord Goring prepares the ground for Jack Worthing and Algernon Moncrieff.

Mabel, like her successors, is shown to be firmly in control of the romantic situation. She is threatening to leave Lord Goring's company, as it is her duty to remain with him, and her duty is a thing she never fulfills, on principle.

LORD GORING: Please don't, Miss Mabel. I have something very particular to say to you.

MABEL CHILTERN (*rapturously*): Oh, is it a proposal?

LORD GORING (*somewhat taken aback*): Well, yes, it is—I am bound to say it is.

MABEL CHILTERN (*with a sigh of pleasure*): I am so glad. That makes the second today. (W572)

Mabel goes on to tell Lord Goring that everyone in London knows she adores him: "It is a public scandal the way I adore you." When Lord Goring confesses that he is not nearly good enough for her, she replies, "I am so glad, darling. I was afraid you were." When he admits to being fearfully extravagant, she matches him, so that they are sure to agree. Finally, when Lord Caversham, Lord Goring's father, threatens to cut him off with a shilling unless he makes Mabel an ideal husband, she intervenes, "An ideal husband! Oh, I don't think I should like that. It sounds like something in the next world." This pair of witty lovers practice a deliberately trivial manner and an elegantly ironic form of speech, in contrast to the serious and moralistic tone that prevails with the married couple of the main plot, Sir Robert and Lady Chiltern. Unfortunately, the complexities of the plot prevent Lord Goring from spending much time on stage with Mabel. As he says at the beginning of Act Four, "I can't find anyone in this house to talk to. And I am full of interesting information. I feel like the latest edition of something or other." He almost needs to be in another play, to have the right people with whom to interact. Perhaps his classic location is the opening exchange in Act Three between him and the Ideal Butler, Phipps, who himself "represents the dominance of form":

LORD GORING: For the future a more trivial buttonhole, Phipps, on Thursday evenings.

PHIPPS: I will speak to the florist, my lord. She has had a loss in her family lately, which perhaps accounts for the lack of triviality your lordship complains of in the buttonhole.

LORD GORING: Extraordinary thing about the lower classes in England—they are always losing their relations.

PHIPPS: Yes, my lord. They are extremely fortunate in that respect. (W554)

Oddly, Shaw praised the "subtle and pervading levity" of this play, while objecting to the heartlessness of its successor. In this exchange with Phipps, we hear the opening notes and rhythms of *The Importance of Being Earnest,* just as the scene between Lord Goring and Mabel is a rehearsal for the proposal of Jack to Gwendolen. Wilde built on these sequences and characters to construct a world that was purely and wholly, instead of only partially, "play" and in which every character participated in the role and stance of the dandy.

One of the artistic problems Wilde grappled with in his earlier comedies was the relationship between the dandies, the aesthetical embodiment of style, and the world to which they were opposed, essentially serious, moralistic, sincere, and, in consequence, verbally and dramatically less colorful. That opposition is an oversimplification, and it can be overcome, or concealed, by subtle acting and imaginative direction, but it helps to explain the reservations that have sometimes been expressed about the theatrical effectiveness of, in particular, *A Woman of No Importance* (a reservation triumphantly dispelled by Philip Prowse's productions in Glasgow and, in 1991, London). Wilde uses the gestures of melodrama and a language heavily indebted to biblical references and cadences for Mrs. Arbuthnot, the wronged woman of no importance, which are echoed and shared by the young American puritan, Hester. In contrast, Lord Illingworth dominates the witty discourse, and shares a common language with the corrupting female dandy, Mrs. Allonby. The conflict between the two philosophies and the two moralities is brilliantly explored. Yet, when Lord Illingworth exits at the close of the play, leaving only his gloves behind, there is a sense of imaginative loss, a diminishing of energy. When Wilde has him say, for example, "A man who can dominate a London dinner-table can dominate the world. The future belongs to the dandy. It is the exquisites who are going to rule," he makes us feel that such a world is conceivable, even desirable—as desirable, certainly, as the privileged existence of upper-class country-house England, with its snobberies and its restrictions, and at least more attractive than the nice, old-fashioned, happy English home which so appals Mrs. Allonby as she examines it, like Gwendolen, through her lorgnette. Wilde, in fact, while dramatizing two worlds, is suggesting a third, an exquisite existence that Lord Illingworth and Mrs. Allonby can indicate and imagine, but from which they are ultimately excluded, except in their speech. As Lady Hunstanton observes after listening to Mrs. Allonby's long definition of the ideal man, "How clever you are, my dear! You never mean a single word you say" (W481).

In *An Ideal Husband,* that exquisite existence is given more solidity by making it a part of a developing relationship and by creating a sense of perspective through Lord Goring's previous encounter with the femme fatale Mrs. Cheveley. The serious people, their rigid moralities softened by experience under the tutorship of the dandy, can be dispatched into the future, to govern England and do good works with rather more insight than they had before (and, incidentally, with the assistance of a fortune created through fraud); the dandies are too intelligent to compromise themselves and prefer to pursue a detached and "trivial" domestic privacy. In the play's first act, Lord Caversham accuses his son of living entirely for pleasure, and the ending endorses his judgment.

In *The Importance of Being Earnest,* Wilde created a world in which all the characters, with one possible exception, are dandies, living, or seeking to live, entirely for pleasure. Algernon asks Jack what brings him up to town, and Jack, as Ernest, replies, "Oh, pleasure, pleasure! What else should bring one anywhere?" (E7). The alternative is to adopt, as guardian, a high moral tone, and a high moral tone can hardly be said to conduce very much to either one's health or one's happiness. Algernon, in pursuit of the same aims, has invented Bunbury and warns Jack that if he ever gets married, he will be very glad to know Bunbury: "A man who marries without knowing Bunbury has a very tedious time of it" (E16). To be Ernest, to know Bunbury, is to construct a life of pleasure, which is at the same time a deception, or at least a fiction, an act of imagination. It is an ideal to which both Gwendolen and Cecily are wholly committed. Gwendolen's pronouncement is definitive: "In matters of grave importance, style, not sincerity, is the vital thing" (E83).

Wilde did not wholly exclude the dark side of existence from his story. Instead, he transformed it into comedy, in the black leather handbag sequence. This is in itself a parody of the traditional recognition scene, which is essentially concerned with relationships. There may be letters, objects, jewels, clothing, or moles involved, but the focus is on individuals and their reunion. Classic instances include the mutual recognition between Sebastian and Viola in *Twelfth Night* and the reunion of the brothers Antipholus with their long-separated parents in *The Comedy of Errors*. The mechanics of the convention have been frequently satirized. Wilde subverted it in an unusual way by making the bag itself the center of attention. Miss Prism, who has shortly before confessed that she once lost a baby, is wholly preoccupied by the bag itself. She identifies it, as though it is a person: "Here is the injury it received through the upsetting of a Gower Street omnibus in younger and happier days." Writing of the 1902 revival, Max Beerbohm criticized the actress playing Prism, Miss Laverton, for omitting "and happier," an apparently redundant phrase that underlines the dazzling self-centeredness of this character.[5] Prism goes on to note the stain on the lining and her initials on the lock. "The bag is undoubtedly mine," she concludes. "I am delighted to have it so unexpectedly restored to me. It has been a great inconvenience being without it all these years" (E100–101). Only after the decorative flourish of the handbag's story does Wilde shift the focus to the abandoned baby. In *A Woman of No Importance* the abandoned mother, Mrs. Arbuthnot, and her baby, Gerald, are handled with pious solemnity. In *The Importance of Being Earnest,* Wilde finds a manner and tone in which he can even indulge in the parody of his own work.

During September and the first part of October, Wilde completed a version of the play, by this time expanded to four acts, and he then began the business of serious negotiation while still based in Worthing. (Remarkably, he had also conceived another scenario, a love tragedy of modern life, which he sent to Alexander and which was eventually written up as *Mr. and Mrs. Daventry,* by Frank Harris.)

Alexander, who was planning a North American tour, wanted to secure American as well as British rights for *The Importance of Being Earnest,* while Wilde, perhaps because he was already committed to one of his American managers, wished to separate them. He wrote to Alexander, "I would like to have my play done by you (I must tell you candidly that the two young men's parts are equally good), but it would be neither for your artistic reputation as a star in the States, nor for my pecuniary advantage, for you to produce it for a couple of nights in each big American town. It would be throwing the thing away." He added, "I can't come up to town, I have no money. . . . Write me your views."[6]

The revised play, with the working title of *Lady Lancing,* was typed at Mrs. Marshall's typewriting agency and stamped "3–25 October 94." Wilde, however, was unable to come to an agreement with Alexander that satisfied them both, and Charles Wyndham, another actor-manager, secured the British rights. However, Alexander's planned winter season fell apart when he found that he had a failure on his hands with Henry James's *Guy Domville.* He knew this on the very first night, 5 January, when James, taking an ill-advised curtain call, was received with a storm of boos and hisses, whereas Wilde, two nights before at the Haymarket, had basked in praise at the opening of *An Ideal Husband.* Alexander had a large clientele of regulars, so that he could run *Guy Domville* for a month while he secured and rehearsed an alternative. He immediately approached Charles Wyndham, who agreed to concede his rights in the new comedy, with the proviso that Wilde would write him another original play. Wyndham had no immediate need for a replacement because of the extended success and run of Henry Arthur Jones's *The Case of Rebellious Susan.* Alexander then persuaded Wilde to compress the four-act version of *The Importance of Being Earnest* into three acts. This was, of course, the form of the scenario that he had first seen. Wilde resisted for a little. "This scene that you feel is superfluous," he later told Alexander, "cost me terrible exhausting labour and heart-rending nerve-racking strain. I assure you on my honour that it must have taken fully five minutes to write."[7]

While the four-act version contains much of interest, Alexander's instincts about the advantages of reducing it to three were undoubtedly correct. The only major cut was a scene in which a solicitor, Gribsby, arrives at the Manor House to serve a writ of attachment for twenty days' imprisonment in Holloway against Ernest Worthing on behalf of the Savoy Hotel, for £762 for a series of suppers, an episode that appears in retrospect to be unnervingly prophetic. Jack, infuriated by Algy's Bunburying, agrees with Dr. Chasuble and Miss Prism that incarceration would do him a great deal of good. Algy is appalled at the prospect: "Well, I really am not going to be imprisoned in the suburbs for having dined in the West End" (W386). Cecily intervenes on Algy's behalf, and Jack relents, on condition that Algy leave by the 3:50 train and that Cecily not speak to him again (unless he asks her a question, since it would be very rude not to answer him). Act Two is set in the morning, and Act Three follows after lunch, with the declaration of love between Algy and Cecily, Gwendolen's arrival, and the girls' discovery of the gross deception that has been practiced on them both. Act Four has a structure similar to that of the ultimate Act Three. The text is generally fuller, with more elaborations and embroideries, some of them memorable. Lady Bracknell advises Dr. Chasuble to be baptized without delay if baptism is, as he professes, a form of new birth: "To be born again would be of considerable advantage to her" (W416). Cecily arranges to meet Algy in the house: "I don't like talking seriously in the open air. It looks so artificial." But the cumulative effect of these diversions is to slow the pace and dilute the comic energy. Wilde rightly trusted Alexander's judgment, and besides, he needed the money. When he came to organize the publication of the play in 1898, the manuscript he had delivered to Alexander formed the basis of the text.

An Ideal Husband opened on 3 January to a warm public and mixed critical reception. Shaw, in the *Saturday Review,* appreciated the play's brilliance, and his comments indicate the strong links between it and *The Importance of Being Earnest:* "In a certain sense Mr. Wilde is to me our only thorough playwright. He plays with everything: with wit, with philosophy, with drama, with actors and audience, with the whole theatre."[8] This review kept Shaw in Wilde's favor as one of "only two dramatic critics in London"; Archer, the other, was struck off Wilde's short list after a less than enthusiastic review in the *National Observer,* though he soon redeemed himself with his reaction to *The Importance of Being Earnest.* Wilde was eager to attend rehearsals of his latest comedy: he had been closely involved in the rehearsal process of all his previous plays. However, Douglas wanted Wilde to accompany him abroad. "I begged him to let me stay to rehearse," Wilde wrote to Ada Leverson, "but so beautiful is his nature that he declined at once."[9] Before he left, he gave an interview to Robert Ross, probably a collaboration, that appeared in the *St. James's Gazette:*

> "Do you think that the critics will understand your new play, which Mr. George Alexander has secured?"
>
> "I hope not."
>
> "I dare not ask, I suppose, if it will please the public?"
>
> "When a play that is a work of art is produced on the stage, what is being tested is not the play, but the stage; when a play that is *not* a work of art is produced on the stage what is being tested is not the play, but the public."
>
> "What sort of play are we to expect?"
>
> "It is exquisitely trivial, a delicate bubble of fancy, and it has its philosophy."
>
> "Its philosophy?"
>
> "That we should treat all the trivial things of life very seriously, and all the serious things of life with sincere and studied triviality."
>
> "You have no leanings towards realism?"
>
> "None whatever. Realism is only a background; it cannot form an artistic motive for a play that is to be a work of art."[10]

On 17 January 1895, Wilde left with Douglas for Algeria, returning alone in time for the final rehearsals. His work on cutting the play must have been completed, though at a fairly late stage, because the typescript submitted for a license to the Lord Chamberlain's office on 30 January is described still as a "comedy (4 acts)," though containing only three. When he came back from North Africa, Wilde is said to have commented, perhaps in reference to the missing act, "Yes, it is quite a good play. I remember I wrote one very like it myself, but it was even more brilliant than this."[11] On 12 February there was a dress rehearsal without scenery. The next day, he wrote to Ada Leverson that the rehearsals were dreary; the cast had colds. There was another, more personal source of anxiety: Douglas's father, the Marquess of Queensberry, was reported to be planning a disturbance on the first night and had sent money to secure himself a ticket. Wilde instructed the business manager to return it, and the police were called in to assist the management in refusing him admission. In the event, Queensberry had to content himself by leaving a grotesque bouquet of vegetables for Wilde at the stagedoor.

On the night of 14 February, St. Valentine's Day,[12] the audience made their way to the theater through a violent snowstorm. Ada Leverson remembered that Wilde was wearing a coat with a black velvet collar, with white gloves, a green scarab ring, a large bunch of seals on a black moire ribbon watch chain hanging from his white waistcoat; his face was a clear red-brown, and a green carnation "bloomed savagely in his button-hole."[13] He watched the play from backstage, perhaps fearing that Queensberry would slip into the theater in disguise, but joined Mrs. Leverson after Act Two in a box where Aubrey Beardsley and Beardsley's sister Mabel were also sitting. By that point, it was clear that the evening was a success, and at the final curtain the play received the most enthusiastic reception of Wilde's career. William Archer wrote in his review, "It is delightful to see, it sends wave after wave of laughter curling and foaming round the theatre." According to Allan Aynesworth, who played Algernon Moncrieff, "In my fifty-three years of acting, I never remember a greater triumph than the first night of *The Importance of Being Earnest*."[14]

PHOTOGRAPHS AND CARTOONS OF
THE ORIGINAL 1895 PRODUCTION OF
THE IMPORTANCE OF BEING EARNEST

George Alexander as Jack, Irene Vanbrugh as Gwendolen, Allan Aynesworth as Algernon. Jack is dictating his address, "The Manor House, Woolton, Hertfordshire," while Algernon consults the Railway Guide. *Sketch,* 20 March 1895.

Rose Leclercq as Lady Bracknell. *Illustrated Sporting and Dramatic News*, 9 March 1895.

Evelyn Millard as Cecily Cardew. *Illustrated Sporting and Dramatic News*, 2 March 1895.

Mrs. George Canninge as Miss Prism, with Cecily. Act 2. *Sketch*, 20 March 1895.

Cecily leading Algernon to ask his "brother's" forgiveness. Act 2. "Uncle Jack, you are not going to refuse your own brother's hand?" *Sketch,* 20 March 1895.

An interpretation of the same encounter by the cartoonist of the *Illustrated Sporting and Dramatic News*, Alfred Bryan.

Frank Dyall as Merriman. "Shall I lay tea here as usual, Miss?" *Sketch*, 20 March 1895.

The Act 2 tea ceremony. Illustrated Sporting and Dramatic News

5

A Question of Class

Although *The Importance of Being Earnest* is ultimately neither a social comedy, like *Lady Windermere's Fan,* nor a satire of contemporary manners, the play functions through the meticulous imitation, and then subversion, of the tribal social customs of upper-class late Victorian society. This was a society where each gesture was significant and was duly noted; where questions of rank, parentage, and wealth were paramount; where custom was enshrined by tradition and by upbringing, slightly modified and refined by fashion; where what you wore, what you ate, where you went, and whom you were seen with defined your status. For those who were not confident about the details, books of etiquette and articles in magazines supplied authoritative advice on the correct way to introduce a viscount's wife to someone of lesser rank, on the proper procedure for proposing marriage, or on the correct time to make a social call in the country. Wilde's plays are rich in such formal ceremonies: the afternoon calls and the "small and early" dance in *Lady Windermere's Fan,* the postdinner sequences in *A Woman of No Importance,* the evening reception in *An Ideal Husband.* In *The Importance of Being Earnest* the scale of the events is more restricted than in those plays, but the details of the rituals are brought into correspondingly sharper focus. An additional tension is achieved by the frequent presence of servants or the expectation that a servant may enter at any moment. It is an essentially public and supremely formal world.

Eating and drinking, major preoccupations of the upper classes and ones that highlighted the conspicuous consumption of the late nineteenth century and required the involvement of a battery of servants, provide one kind of structure. A comparison between the three-act and the four-act versions reveals that these activities loomed even larger in earlier drafts, with the addition of lunch to punctuate the day in the country and Cecily's admission that her Uncle Jack has been ordered by his London doctor to have pâté de foie gras sandwiches and 1889 champagne at noon. In the final version, Act One opens with Algernon checking on the arrangements for entertaining his aunt to tea, and closes with a glass of sherry. Wilde elevated the cutting of a cucumber sandwich to a science, a proposition both absurd and trivial yet entirely serious. It is part of a pattern of ceremony in which both Jack's inscribed cigarette case and the afternoon post will be presented on a silver salver. There are also the references to dining at Willis's and the details of Lady Bracknell's dinner party and evening reception. Act Two contains the incisively aggressive tea ceremony, in which Cecily insults Gwendolen with lumps of sugar and a slice of cake, and the matching tussle between Jack and Algernon over the muffins and tea cake. The interrogations and revelations of Act Three leave little space for food, though it begins with the men's offstage act of repentance in eating muffins and contains Jack's outraged reconstruction of Algernon drinking an entire pint bottle of Perrier-Jouet champagne under an assumed name. In terms of etiquette, however, there is Lady Bracknell's minute scrutiny of Cecily's deportment, and the play closes with the authority of the entry in a standard book of British tribal reference, the Army List.

The common factor in all these episodes is appearance: "They have been eating muffins. That looks like repentance." Lady Bracknell's comment on her nephew could be taken as the play's motto: "Algernon is an extremely, I may almost say an ostentatiously, eligible young man. He has nothing, but he looks everything. What

42

more can one desire?" (E92). Inspecting Cecily, she demands the side view: "Yes, quite as I expected. There are distinct social possibilities in your profile. The two weak points in our age are its want of principle and its want of profile. The chin a little higher, dear. Style largely depends on the way the chin is worn. They are worn very high, just at present" (E90–91). As she has pronounced earlier, "We live, I regret to say, in an age of surfaces."

Surface, style, and fashion reign in this play, in physical appearance, in posture, in gesture, in speech. When Lane hands Algernon the cucumber sandwiches on a salver, Algernon first inspects them, before taking two. We assume that he might send them back, like a corked bottle of wine, had they proved unsatisfactory. When Jack enters, a stage direction in George Alexander's working copy indicates that Jack brings hat, stick, and gloves with him into the room rather than leaving them with Lane outside, implying that he is making only a short visit. However, when he notices that Algy is eating, he sits on the sofa—without being invited to do so—and begins to pull off his gloves. Each successive gesture marks his increasing confidence as prospective suitor. The significance of the number of cups and the cucumber sandwiches prompts him to ask, "Who is coming to tea?" Before Gwendolen even arrives, Jack has begun to eat the bread and butter intended for her. As Algy remarks, "You need not eat as if you were going to eat it all. You behave as if you were married to her already" (E9).

When Jack is proposing to Gwendolen, he protests, "You know what I have got to say to you." Gwendolen replies, "Yes, but you don't say it." The form is paramount, and as Gwendolen herself comments, men often propose for practice in order to perfect it. "I hope you will always look at me just like that," she adds, "especially when there are other people present" (E25). Each action takes on a new dimension if there is an audience, and in a world of high social gesture, there almost always is. The proposal might be assumed to be one of this society's few private moments. When Lady Bracknell intrudes and orders Mr. Worthing to rise from his "semi-recumbent posture," she adds significantly, "It is most indecorous." Gwendolen, begging her mother to retire, points out the social lapse: "This is no place for you." However, she then highlights the artificiality of the occasion by explaining that "Mr. Worthing has not quite finished yet." Lady Bracknell finally stamps her authority on the real mechanics of betrothal: "When you do become engaged to some one, I, or your father, should his health permit him, will inform you of the fact." In such a society, the pulling-off of a glove and the kneeling before a loved one are part of a continuum, an elaborate dance of timing and style and gesture, and the women are the most adept practitioners and skilled interpreters.

A heightened sense of performance is the logical extension of the whole business of etiquette: manners are elevated to the status of art. When Jack tells Gwendolen, "We must get married at once," naturally using her first name, all Gwendolen has to do to indicate her surprise is to reply, with all the hauteur of her mother, "Married, Mr. Worthing?" The use of his surname at once returns the relationship to one of appropriate distance and formality, regardless of the fact that she has already declared passionate love for her own Ernest. No properly brought-up girl would allow herself to be addressed by a man by her Christian name before her engagement. In Act Three, once Lady Bracknell has given her premature consent to the marriage between Algernon and Cecily, she invites Cecily to kiss her and to address her as Aunt Augusta. Lady Bracknell's consent, of course, should strictly be dependent on her husband's agreement, but Lady Bracknell, like all the characters, bends etiquette and manners to her own desires, recognizing the importance of society and its customs but reinventing them to her own particular design. In this way, Wilde exploited the detailed pattern of social gesture that dominated the lives of the Victorian upper classes, inviting recognition from the predominantly upper-class audience in the stalls and boxes or fascinated observation by the less wealthy in the pit and the gallery. He then proceeded to elaborate and to subvert the system, creating a highly self-conscious texture that unfolds within a slightly surreal, dreamlike world, a world clearly founded on contemporary custom but not bound by its laws and restrictions. The intention is not primarily to satirize the ridiculous nature of some social rituals and taboos, though that may be one intermittent effect, but to infuse them with a new and independent life.

One example of the cumulative mocking of convention is the christening motif, introduced by Jack during his Act One proposal scene with Gwendolen, in response to her declaration that the name Jack produces absolutely no vibrations: "Gwendolen, I must get christened at once—I mean we must get married at once." The ceremonies are treated as interchangeable. In Act Two, the subject arises in juxtaposition to the announcement of Ernest's death, linked by Canon Chasuble's all-purpose sermon on the meaning of the manna in the wilderness, which can be adapted to almost any occasion, joyful or distressing: christenings, confirmations, days of humiliation, or festal days. Chasuble is perfectly agreeable to perform the job. He regards it as an interesting rarity: "The sprinkling, and, indeed, the immersion of adults is a perfectly canonical practice" (E53). Any serious significance of what is the most important sacrament of the Christian church is wholly ignored, a dismissal put into definitive perspective by Lady Bracknell's two imperious pronouncements on the subject in Act Three. First, to Chasuble's explanation that both Jack and Algernon have expressed a desire for immediate baptism: "At their age? The idea is grotesque and irreligious. Algernon, I forbid you to be baptized. I will not hear of such excesses. Lord Bracknell would be highly displeased if he learned that that was the way in which you wasted your time and money" (E96). The closing addition "and money" is revealing, for the clergyman's fee for a christening would be derisory, which makes the financial consideration absurd; nevertheless, Lady Bracknell's comments offer an insight into the money-dominated scale of values of the upper classes and is an instinctive signal as to how they regard the functions of the established church. Her second statement, in answer to Jack's enquiry as to whether he had been christened before being left in Miss Prism's handbag, is majestically assertive: "Every luxury that money could buy, including christening, had been lavished on you by your fond and doting parents" (E102). The elevation of christening, the simplest of ceremonies available even to poor Jenkins the carter, to the ranks of luxury is the ultimate accolade of a consumer society.

The most telling image of the class system that Wilde depicts, celebrates, and mocks is the role of the servants. Algernon's statement near the beginning of Act One, significantly shared with the wealthy audience, sets the tone: "Lane's views on marriage seem somewhat lax. Really, if the lower orders don't set us a good example, what on earth is the use of them? They seem, as a class, to have absolutely no sense of moral responsibility." Their use, of course, is to make the lives of the upper classes comfortable; and the habits, champagne drinking, and the morality of the "lower orders" as represented by Lane seem modeled on those of his employer. When Lady Bracknell arrives, he demonstrates that he is a consummate liar:

> ALGERNON (*picking up empty plate in horror*): Good heavens! Lane! Why are there no cucumber sandwiches? I ordered them specially.
>
> LANE (*gravely*): There were no cucumbers in the market this morning, sir. I went down twice.
>
> ALGERNON: No cucumbers!
>
> LANE: No, sir. Not even for ready money. (E19)

It comes as no surprise, therefore, that Lane is fully aware of Algernon's double life and needs no other instruction than "I'm going Bunburying" to make his intentions clear. To Algernon's vapid "I hope tomorrow will be a fine day," Lane replies, "It never is, sir," illustrating the perversely subtle nature of the master-servant relationship. To be negative, or realistic, and so invite and indulge the master's rebuke, is a much subtler and more elegant way of providing a good service than an obsequious agreement. Lane's parting shot, "I do my best to give satisfaction, sir" (E40), summarizes Lane's exquisite understanding of his role.

If Lane is a development of Phipps, the ideal manservant of *An Ideal Husband*, Merriman, at the Manor House, has, dramatically, a less marked personality. His function is to make announcements and to supervise the mechanics of English upper-class life: tea under the yew tree, champagne when requested, luggage and transport. Yet, his role is far from neutral. He has seven entrances in Act Two, and Frank

Dyall, who played the part in the first production, recalled that the first, the announcement that Ernest Worthing has just driven over from the station, received the loudest and most sustained laugh that he had ever experienced, culminating in a round of applause.[1] He is party to the sequence of contradictions about the dogcart. He presides over the teatime battle of etiquette between Cecily and Gwendolen, fully aware of the implications, but saying nothing. Finally, he has the presence of mind to cough in warning when he announces the arrival of Lady Bracknell. As with Lane, the comedy is grounded in his absolute aplomb and in the lack of personal reaction to anything he sees. He behaves as if the events of the day are entirely normal, making a comment on the artificiality of this kind of life by his very lack of comment. In Nicholas Hytner's 1993 London production, the role of Merriman was played by Hugh Munro. He moved with extreme slowness, conveying by his infinite patience a kind of wearied acceptance of the demands placed upon him by the whims of his employer. As he shuffled about his tasks, he seemed, like Firs in Chekhov's *The Cherry Orchard*, to emphasize the fragility of the social structure.

The audience's awareness of the class system and, in particular, of the position of the lower classes is maintained throughout the action by a number of references, yet one more leitmotiv in the play's rich texture. Because it contains so little "real" substance, there is ample opportunity to refer to the constant preoccupations of the English aristocracy. The keynote is sounded, appropriately, by Lady Bracknell in her strictures on modern education: "Fortunately in England, at any rate, education produces no effect whatsoever. If it did, it would prove a serious danger to the upper classes, and probably lead to acts of violence in Grosvenor Square" (E27). During the comparatively stable decade of the nineties, acts of violence might seem a comfortable joke to share with the well-dressed audience of the St. James's Theatre; but the century had seen sufficient social unrest for there to be a rational fear buried within it. To the announcement that Bunbury was quite exploded, she retorts, "Exploded! Was he the victim of a revolutionary outrage? I was not aware that Mr. Bunbury was interested in social legislation. If so, he is well punished for his morbidity" (E87). The class that Lady Bracknell represents is one that will make no compromises to protect their way of life and their incomes. No approval is given of "the modern sympathy with invalids": "Health is the primary duty of life." In this precept, Wilde, through Lady Bracknell, voices the same attitude as the inhabitants of Samuel Butler's *Erewhon,* wherein criminals receive treatment at the hands of "straighteners" but invalids are punished severely by imprisonment or, in extreme cases, by the death penalty. It is the philosophy of the post-Darwinian era, where the strongest and healthiest thrive and the inferior classes are kept in their places by an infinite variety of strategies.

Canon Chasuble and Miss Prism are also, though in a different way, servants. Chasuble, as rector, would most probably have been appointed to his office by Jack Worthing, the substantial local landowner. He will christen on demand, infants or adults, and preach to order. Miss Prism, her imaginative dimension locked up in abandoned fiction, has been pushing perambulators and giving German lessons to young ladies to earn a living. The lowly place she occupies within society, concealed by the politeness of Cecily and Jack and the attentions of Canon Chasuble, is brought glaringly into the open by Lady Bracknell, whose terrifying and repeated form of address— "Prism!"—relegates her, without the "Miss," to the ranks of a housemaid. By his inclusion of Prism and Chasuble, however much they may be stock figures of comedy, Wilde broadened the frame of reference in a way that he had never previously explored in his plays, except fleetingly in *A Woman of No Importance.*

Lady Bracknell herself is an example of the English class system at work, continually redefining and recreating itself. Maggie Smith, under Nicholas Hytner's direction, developed this aspect, based on her revelation in Act Three: "When I married Lord Bracknell I had no fortune of any kind. But I never dreamed for a moment of allowing that to stand in my way" (E91). John Peter in the *Sunday Times* commented that Maggie Smith's performance reminds you

> that Lady Bracknell had risen from nowhere in particular to the upper classes without setting foot in the intervening area of meritocracy. On the way, she has taken on the protective colouring and the belligerent assumptions of her host-class, including those

casual little bursts of vulgarity of which only the British aristocracy is capable. What gives her away is the impertinent look of
appraisal with which she scrutinises new arrivals. This is not the
practised glance of the true upper-class matriarch, who takes in
everything at the blink of an eye, but the ruthless inquisitorial
stare of the middle-class climber who has had to learn what to
look for.[2]

Lady Bracknell is transfixed when it is revealed that Cecily Cardew has
£130,000 in government securities. Just as her own fortunes have been
made by an advantageous marriage, so her nephew Algernon, who
looks everything but has nothing, and her daughter Gwendolen will be
offered the true security of money. Wilde, himself a parvenu among
the English aristocracy, understood only too well the key relationship
between class and money, and his exposure and exploitation of it is
one of the sources of comedy within this play.

6

Names and Places

The names that Wilde finally chose for his characters have acquired enormous resonance over the century. They carry a wide range of connotation, from the public to the intensely private. The title, with its pun on Earnest/Ernest (a joke that the *Graphic* advised Wilde to discard and on which Wilde's fellow playwright Sydney Grundy unfairly commented, "Could any but a diseased brain have conceived so contemptible a pun?"), at once draws attention to the importance of names. The word *importance* had already figured twice in Wilde's work, most prominently in *A Woman of No Importance,* where the phrase is also used to end the first act and then reversed in the play's final words, spoken by the woman of "no importance" herself, Mrs. Arbuthnot: "Oh! no one. No one in particular. A man of no importance." It had also featured in the epigraphs to Wilde's essay "The Critic as Artist" (published in *Intentions,* 1891). The first part of this dialogue has the additional description "with some remarks upon the importance of doing nothing," and the second part, "with some remarks upon the importance of discussing everything." The two characters who conduct the dialogue are named Gilbert and Ernest, and the dialogue, set in the library of a house in Piccadilly, begins with

Gilbert at the piano. One further context in which Wilde explored the "importance" idea was in "Phrases and Philosophies for the Use of the Young," his contribution to the *Chameleon:* "In all unimportant matters, style, not sincerity, is the essential. In all important matters, style, not sincerity, is the essential" (W1244).

In a play about surfaces, labels assume a special significance. The name Ernest holds the promise of a proper Victorian seriousness and is therefore an appropriate object of the fantasies of a Gwendolen or a Cecily, should they be conventionally serious and high-minded young women. For Gwendolen, it is "the only really safe name"; for Cecily, there is something in it "that seems to inspire absolute confidence. I pity any poor married woman whose husband is not called Ernest." At the same time, the name suggests for each a rather more sensuous and dangerous dimension: for Gwendolen, "it produces vibrations"; for Cecily, the name has delicious associations with a younger brother "who was very wicked and bad," a combination somehow indicating both unmentionable depravity and the simplest kind of morality from a children's rhyme. To be Ernest, then, is to be something other than what one seems.

Wilde had already played with the name's potential ambivalence in *A Woman of No Importance,* in which Mrs. Allonby, the female dandy, is married to an Ernest in whom she has been horribly deceived. Lady Stutfield asks her what was the wrong thing Mr. Allonby did, and Mrs. Allonby replies, "When Ernest and I were engaged, he swore to me positively on his knees that he had never loved anyone before in the whole course of his life. I was very young at the time, so I didn't believe him, I needn't tell you. Unfortunately, however, I made no inquiries of any kind till after I had been actually married four or five months. I found out then what he had told me was perfectly true. And that sort of thing makes a man so absolutely uninteresting" (W480). For Mrs. Allonby, a good, pure, and inexperienced husband is an insult to her personality. The potential husbands of *The Importance of Being Earnest,* largely invented by Gwendolen and Cecily, convey through their common name a much more fascinating allure. "I have known several Jacks, and they all, without exception, were more than usually plain. Besides, Jack is a notorious domesticity for John! And I pity any woman who is married to a man called John. She would probably never be allowed to know the entrancing pleasure of a single moment's solitude." When Gwendolen concludes, "The only really safe name is Ernest" (E24), she implies a much more interesting *lack* of safety. She seems unfazed by the knowledge that General Moncrieff, Jack's father (and her uncle by marriage), was "essentially a man of peace, except in his domestic life."

The name's ironic potential was seized on by Samuel Butler, who used it for his innocently wicked hero Ernest Pontifex, in *The Way of All Flesh* (published in 1903, though begun thirty years earlier). Timothy d'Arch Smith, in *Love in Earnest,*[1] has argued that Ernest was, in addition, a coded reference to homosexuality, one of a number of allusions to Wilde's particular current circle of friends within the play. Another such probable allusion is the Lady Bloxham mentioned by Lady Bracknell in Act One: Jack Bloxam was the young editor of an Oxford undergraduate magazine, *The Chameleon,* in which work by both Lord Alfred Douglas and Wilde appeared in 1894. But it is also worth recalling that the husband of Wilde's closest woman friend of this time, Ada Leverson, was named Ernest. The name has a comic pattern of slightly absurd and sometimes risqué association for the English; its abbreviated form, Ernie, who "drove the fastest milk cart in the West," has been celebrated in the comedian Benny Hill's music-hall song.

Jack, who, it transpires, naturally is Ernest, also conveys seriousness and worthiness through his adopted surname of Worthing, highly suitable for a justice of the peace. He has acquired a "gravity of demeanour," according to Miss Prism, especially to be commended in one so comparatively young, though Cecily correctly interprets this gravity as a sign of boredom. Worthing, the Sussex seaside resort where Wilde was on holiday with his wife, his two young sons, and their governess when working on the play, is one of four Sussex place-names referred to, the others being Shoreham, Lancing, and Brighton. Wilde often used place-names with personal associations for his characters. Lord Goring in *An Ideal Husband* recalls Goring-on-Thames, where Wilde was staying when he began that play; Lady Hunstanton in *A Woman of No Importance* derives from a Norfolk holiday. In this case, with three of the four references in Act One, there may be a submerged reference to the seaside world of boardinghouse summers, a common setting for English farce. Characteristically, this expectation is raised only to be denied by the style of the play.

Jack Worthing's younger brother, Algernon Moncrieff, has a distinctly more trivial and aristocratic ring. The name Moncrieff was a relatively late change from Montford, a name Wilde had already used in *An Ideal Husband*. In the first scenario, the London friend was called Lord Alfred Rufford, a minor character in *A Woman of No Importance;* Wilde may have considered this name to be too close a correspondence with Lord Alfred Douglas for comfort. The Douglas connection, however, is obliquely referred to in Lady Bracknell's name, Bracknell being the home of Douglas's mother, the Marchioness of Queensberry. The offstage Lord Bracknell must be a baron or viscount, a rank indicated by the courtesy title of "the Honourable" given to Gwendolen Fairfax. Cecily Cardew's names record Wilde's acquaintance with the Cardew family, whose daughter Cicely was born in 1893: two of her uncles were at Magdalen College, Oxford, with Wilde, and her grandfather was co-incidentally a director of the London, Brighton, and South Coast Railway, which ran the trains to Worthing. Cécile is the name of the ingenue in Alfred de Musset's comedy *Il ne faut jurer de rien* (Never swear to anything), which has been viewed as a possible source for *The Importance of Being Earnest*.[2]

The servants' names, Lane and Merriman, were originally Lane and Mathews, the names of Wilde's publishers, according to Max Beerbohm. Wilde was in the middle of an acrimonious dispute with them during the autumn of 1894, but he relented where Mathews was concerned. The final category of names belongs to the more broadly drawn, less refined characters, Chasuble and Prism, neither of whom turn out to be what they seem, or sound like, chaste and prissy. A chasuble is a special robe worn by priests when celebrating the Eucharist, which places Chasuble as a member of the High Church movement, which Wilde encountered at Oxford, and, together with his special interest in the church fathers, suggests the kind of clergyman who might well have taken a vow of celibacy. "Prism," which sounds like "prison," is a reference to Dickens's *Little Dorrit*, in which the governess, Mrs. General, says, "Papa, potatoes, poultry, prunes, and prism, are all very good words for the lips: especially prunes and prism." A Miss Prunes and Prism is proverbial for a prim and prissy person, and the other meanings connected with geometry and optics are wonderfully appropriate for a governess. The touch of cruelty in Lady Bracknell's description of Prism as "a female of repellent aspect" may derive from the "quite impossible" and "horrid ugly Swiss governess"[3] who had been looking after Wilde's children. Miss Prism's name is the only one surviving from Wilde's first scenario, where she was described as a "dragon of propriety."

The settings of the play indicate wealth: the wealth of the late Victorian upper classes, whose money is inherited or acquired by judicious marriages, rather than directly earned, and in which the main characters float on an effortless tide of luxury, waited on by dignified, even (in the case of Lane) dandified servants. Algernon's flat is in Half Moon Street, in the heart of the West End of London, within easy reach of restaurants, theaters, and gentlemen's clubs. It is "luxuriously and artistically" furnished. On a Thursday night, at dinner, eight bottles of champagne between three people were "entered as having been consumed," some of them, Algernon implies, by the servants. Jack Worthing has taken rooms in the fashionable Albany, off Piccadilly; this was another private reference, as Wilde's homosexual friend George Ives had rooms at E.4, The Albany. Jack's Mayfair house in Belgrave Square is let. His country place, the Manor House, Woolton, Hertfordshire, is more conveniently placed for London than the remoter Shropshire of Algernon's guess. Cecily Cardew's grandfather had three resonant addresses in London, Surrey, and Fife; three addresses, as Lady Bracknell remarks, "always inspire confidence, even in tradesmen." A. B. Walkley, reviewing the original production, commented that "a root-idea of farce like this requires an aristocratic *milieu* for due expansion, an atmosphere of wealth and leisure; Mr. Wilde's people would be monsters, had they not several thousands a year, handles to their names, Grandisonian butlers, and dresses from the Rue de la Paix." Certainly, the sense of expansive luxury and infinite leisure is a crucial part of Wilde's idealized world. Yet, it would have struck an immediate chord with the fashionable first-nighters, who for the most part inhabited such a world. The Duke and Duchess of Fife, for example, were regular attendees at St. James's Theatre openings.

Wilde deliberately constructed a pattern of allusion to real places and institutions. Some of these are relatively mundane, such as Victoria Station and a Gower Street omnibus, but some have private associations for Wilde: the Grand Hotel in Paris was one of his favorite haunts, as was Willis's restaurant in King Street, just round the corner from the St. James's Theatre. But, more crucially, the references connect the world of the play to the world of the audience, neatly, if misleadingly, suggesting that they are one and the same. Some of the audience would dine at Willis's after the performance, as Wilde's friend Ada Leverson did after the first night. Others, or rather the males, might move on to the Empire music hall in Leicester Square, a notorious rendezvous for prostitutes, where they could see a "Grand Ballet" featuring the premiere danseuse Helène Cornalba in *Round the Town.*

Victorian England was an England with an empire, which provided careers, markets, and new lands to absorb the surplus population. The text reminds us of this dimension by two references. First, there is the question of Algy's emigrating, Jack's latest reason, so Cecily informs Algy, for traveling up to town. Algy is going to the far side of the world, to Australia, where he will not need any neckties. Australia, being both inaccessible and rough, was a favorite destination for wayward younger sons or brothers. At the end of the play, we learn that General Moncrieff's health suffered from the Indian climate: his career in the Indian Army had cost him his life, not on the battlefield but the sickbed, and no doubt that of his wife too, Lady Bracknell's "poor sister" Mrs. Moncrieff.

The Importance of Being Earnest is usually seen as particularly "English"; certainly Wilde, as a cosmopolitan Irishman with a position of privileged familiarity, mocks many aspects of the English class system and way of life. The two cultures that he uses for comic perspective are those of Germany and France. German, as Lady Bracknell remarks, "sounds a thoroughly respectable language," and appropriately forms part of Cecily's curriculum. The German royal family was closely related to the British monarchy, and Germany was therefore associated with worthiness and seriousness. But Cecily feels that German is not a becoming language: she knows perfectly well that she looks quite plain after her German lesson. French, however, verges on the indecent. Lady Bracknell cannot possibly allow French songs to be played at her receptions. Ernest "dies" in Paris of a severe chill and reportedly expresses a desire to be buried there. As Chasuble laments, "I fear that hardly points to any very serious state of mind at the last." The two European contrasts provide an additional dimension to the pervasive opposition between the serious and the trivial.

The play moves from London to the country. The contrast between these locations is conventional in English comedies of manners, such as those of Congreve or Sheridan, which can occasionally be sensed in the background echoes and shadows. Earlier in the nineteenth century, Boucicault's *London Assurance* revived the traditional dichotomy. In *The Importance of Being Earnest,* however, the prevailing tone is relentlessly urban and sophisticated, as smart as Gwendolen Fairfax's appearance. The shift to the country, which might indicate a change of tone to something more innocent and pastoral, is deceptive. In the four-act version, the tea-table scene was set indoors, its correct location according to Camille Paglia, in her commentary on the play in *Sexual Personae:* "The drawing-room, its proper place, is the eighteenth-century salon of the androgyne of manners."[4] However, as in Act One of *A Woman of No Importance,* Wilde contrived to suggest that the country-house garden is as fully constructed and aesthetic an environment as any interior. Basket chairs; a table covered with books; and the appearance of Merriman and a footman with salver, tablecloth, and plate stand contrive to turn the "natural" into a comfortable but strictly temporary extension of the house. Even Cecily's watering of the roses appears as an aesthetic gesture, as though she is a figure in a pastel by Watteau, and she seems fully conscious of the possible comparison. She is, she informs Gwendolen, "very fond of being looked at." The garden, like Cecily's diary, has only the deceptive appearance of being natural. Cecily's diary "is simply a very young girl's record of her own thoughts and impressions, and consequently meant for publication." Cecily, who is eighteen but admits to twenty when she goes to evening parties, will soon be taking her place in London society, along with Lady Lancing and Lady Dumbleton. The Manor House, Woolton, Hertfordshire, will not, Wilde suggests, be seeing much more of any of these characters. In the scenario, the Guardian only mollifies his betrothed by promising never to live in the country: "The country is demoralising: it makes you respectable. 'The simple fare at the Savoy: the quiet life in Piccadilly: the solitude of Mayfair is what you need, etc.'" Although these lines did not appear in the final text, the unspoken messages of the play promote an urban, fin de siècle, and sophisticated artifice. Yet, the context in which this idyll unfolds is recognizably the same world as the audience inhabits, with the same clothes, manners, titles, and geography.

7

Characters

With a play so concentrated upon the fashioning of a glittering and polished surface, it may be dangerous to discuss the "characters" in too great detail, for such an approach might suggest that Wilde was aiming to create individuals who are psychologically convincing or somehow related to, or relatable to, "reality." More emphatically than in most comedy, these characters are overtly fictional, dramatic constructs who belong far more to the traditions and conventions of drama than they do to their counterparts in "real life." Of course, since they are acted by men and women, and not by marionettes, they look deceptively like inhabitants of upper-class Victorian England in the 1890s, itself a self-consciously modern decade in Wilde's view. They share their manners, appetites, and language, or, rather, they behave and speak in a way that would be instantly recognizable by their predominantly upper-class and middle-class audiences. Yet, as has already been argued, they exude an intense self-awareness about what they say and do and about how they look. Almost everything they say is spoken for effect, almost nothing is spontaneous or unconsidered, and as a consequence, they continually draw attention to their artificiality. Lady Bracknell may utter regret that "we live . . . in an age of surfaces," but she and all the other characters rise triumphantly to the challenge.

Wilde was extraordinarily economical in the number of roles he employed in *The Importance of Being Earnest,* in contrast to the many minor parts he made use of in his earlier plays. The enforced reduction from four acts to three acts is partly responsible, but the increased compression is a distinct advantage, sharpening the strong sense of pattern while never seeming to be restrictive, for Wilde has great skill in sketching his frame of reference by creating rapid vignettes of offstage people: the insignificant Lord Bracknell; Mary Farquhar, who flirts with her own husband across the dinner table; and Lady Harbury, whose hair has turned quite gold from grief. Wilde created his world with only nine characters: two pairs of lovers, the bachelor "friends" Algernon and Jack and the single young women Gwendolen and Cecily; a pair of older, mildly grotesque guardian figures, Miss Prism (education) and Canon Chasuble (religion); two manservants; and the formidable solo figure of Lady Bracknell, aunt, parent, Gorgon, and dea ex machina.

Algernon and Jack are subtly contrasted, first, of course, by name. The "seriousness" and worthiness of John Worthing, justice of the peace and guardian of Cecily, owner of country and town houses, is opposed to the elegant frivolity suggested by Algernon Moncrieff, a distinction bolstered by a swiftly established age difference sufficient for Jack to be able to say to Algernon, "Why such reckless extravagance in one so young?" This difference tends to be more marked in stage performance. Writing about the 1982 English National Theatre production, Michael Billington drew attention in his *Guardian* review[1] to the contrast between the dry formality of Martin Jarvis's whey-faced Jack, with his "wing collar, cruel specs and severe swept back hair," and the "floppy-cravatted, curly-haired" insouciance of Nigel Havers as Algernon. The same variation in gravity is expressed in Anthony Asquith's classic film version, in the contrast between the more serious demeanor of Michael Redgrave's Ernest, aided by his moustache, and the fresh-faced, debonair manner of Michael Denison as Algy. As the first act unfolds, however, it becomes clear that

Algernon and Jack have several things in common, most noticeably their commitment to deception. Algernon has invented a fictitious friend, the invalid Bunbury, whose perilous state of health enables his creator to escape from London and disappear to the country or to wriggle out of a tedious dinner engagement whenever it suits him. Jack has not only conceived a younger brother who gets into the most dreadful scrapes as an excuse for leaving his serious duties in Hertfordshire but actually impersonates him. He takes rooms in the fashionable Albany, in Piccadilly, and even has visiting cards inscribed with his assumed name and address. In the dual roles of Ernest in town and Jack in the country, he is, as Algernon comments, one of the most advanced Bunburyists he knows. Profiting from Jack's example, Algernon himself impersonates the fictional younger brother Ernest; and just as Jack is prepared to get rid of Ernest when his usefulness has expired, so Algernon will dispose of Bunbury. This commitment to a double life marks their instinctive brotherhood. In their appetites for champagne, cucumber sandwiches, and muffins, as in their adoration of Gwendolen and Cecily, the two pursue closely parallel courses.

It is sometimes objected that at the close of the play Wilde loses his hitherto unerring grip on the plot's symmetry by leaving Algernon with his original name, just as Demetrius, in *A Midsummer Night's Dream,* remains under the influence of the love potion whereas Lysander has been treated with the antidote. But Algernon has been changed in one important respect, in becoming recognized as Jack's wicked younger brother, if not finally Ernest, while Jack, in assuming his rightful and original name of Ernest, has inevitably shifted status to become an older brother. During the course of the play they have both taken on the role of Ernest and younger brother, a complicated double act that they now share between them. To impersonate the same fiction suggests a closeness that echoes previous explorations of twins, such as the brothers Antipholus in *The Comedy of Errors* or the more compli-cated scenario of Goldoni's *The Venetian Twins,* in which one actor plays two contrasting twin brothers, one from the town and one from the country (one of whom is killed off at the close); there are, too, echoes of the related older-younger brother relationship of Oliver and Orlando in *As You Like It* or the two Surfaces in Sheridan's *The School for Scandal.* The family ties in this fictional world are disturbingly close: Jack will become engaged to his first cousin, while Algernon seeks to marry his brother's ward, a kind of cousin by adoption.

The differentiation between Gwendolen and Cecily is, superficially, more marked. Gwendolen, rapidly established during Act One, is supremely confident, sophisticated, and smart. Alone of the four lovers, she has a secure and traditional family context, with both parents living, even if it is a context from which she struggles to escape. Her milieu is London. As her mother remarks, "A girl with a simple, unspoiled nature, like Gwendolen, could hardly be expected to reside in the country" (E28). Gwendolen holds brisk and forthright views about the course and conduct of her future emotional life: "Whatever influence I ever had over mamma, I lost at the age of three. But although she may prevent us from becoming man and wife, and I may marry someone else, and marry often, nothing that she can possibly do can alter my eternal devotion to you" (E38). She is even prepared to risk an excursion into the country, with its tedium of interesting walks and flowers, to be with her betrothed.

Cecily, marooned in the country, protected by guardian and governess, is first introduced to the audience in a garden setting, decoratively watering the roses. (In the original production, Evelyn Millard distributed "what looked like real water" over the "mimic garden": the water was silver sand.) Yet, Cecily is soon revealed as fully capable of looking after herself, tempting Miss Prism to a walk in the park with Dr. Chasuble through her fiction of a headache—"I felt instinctively that you had a headache"—and making her views on her enforced education crystal clear: "Horrid Political Economy! Horrid Geography! Horrid, horrid German!" (E45). She has, it soon transpires, been developing her own sentimental education in private, as she reveals in her second tête-à-tête with Algernon. Her diary and letters record the full course of her passionate affair with Ernest. She shares the habit of keeping a "sensational" diary with Gwendolen, who never travels without it. As the plot unfolds, the similarities between the two girls become more arresting than their differences. There is a soft sibilance to the name Cecily Cardew, in keeping with her "sadly simple" dress and hair, which "seems almost as Nature might have left it." The crisper sound of the name Gwendolen Fairfax, the lorgnette through which she inspects the world, her glossy and achieved perfection—"I never change except in my affections"—provide the external contrast. Their impressive persistence, their ability to manipulate their lovers and outwit their guardians, and, above all, their spirited commitment to their imagined ideals mark an essential sisterhood. They are, without proclaiming it, Wilde's subtle contribution to the idea of the New Woman. Cecily, because she appears less sophisticated and has been compelled hitherto to inhabit a largely imaginative world, turns out to be the more artful and consummate practitioner. Gwendolen, like Mabel Chiltern in *An Ideal Husband,* has had more experience of the ways of the world. She is well aware, for example, that "men often propose for practice. I know my brother Gerald does. All my girl-friends tell me so" (E25).

Whereas all four lovers move within the same style and register of language, Wilde provides a contrast, most noticeably in Act Two, through the idiosyncratic pedantry of Miss Prism and Canon Chasuble. Their comic names and pattern of speech create an immediate affinity. As governess and rector, they are the representatives and preachers of moral precept. Miss Prism speaks like a character from an eighteenth-century novel, with expansive syntax, judicious qualification, and polysyllabic words: "Your guardian enjoys the best of health, and his gravity of demeanour is especially to be commended in one so comparatively young as he is" (E42). She delivers, with considerable relish, the more judgmental aspect of Victorian society and religion: "As a man sows, so shall he reap." At the same time, she reveals every now and again a more willful, hedonistic side to her nature, as in her admission that she wrote a three-volume novel in earlier days. Occasionally, too, her command of language slips, indicating a subconscious train of thought at odds with her respectable exterior. One example occurs, significantly, in her reference to her novel: "The manuscript unfortunately was abandoned." When Cecily starts at "abandoned," Miss Prism corrects herself: "I used the word in the sense of lost or mislaid," simultaneously signaling her understanding of its other sense of "morally loose" (E43).

Characters

Canon Chasuble, a celibate, a Doctor of Divinity steeped in the writings of the church fathers, begins by adopting a suitably moral and clerical tone: "I hope, Cecily, you are not inattentive." He, too, however, soon lapses into a vein of inappropriate connotation: "Were I fortunate enough to be Miss Prism's pupil, I would hang upon her lips." At a glare from Miss Prism, he attempts to correct himself, but compounds the error by the seemingly innocent "birds and bees" connotation of his explanation: "I spoke metaphorically.—My metaphor was drawn from bees" (E44). His next compliment is to allude to "Egeria and her pupil." Egeria was the nymph who instructed Numa Pompilius, the second king of Rome, and so her name became a proverbial synonym for any wise counselor. The comment conveniently allows Miss Prism to reveal her Christian name, Laetitia, which Chasuble, as a Latinist, knows means "joy"; and his next gloss, "a classical allusion merely, drawn from the Pagan authors," hints that his mind runs on secular lines just as much as on religion. Miss Prism responds to what has clearly been a suppressed sexual invitation by calling him "dear Doctor" and using her fictional headache not as an excuse to avoid a sexual encounter but as a positive reason why she should take a stroll with him, leaving Cecily to continue with her education on her own. In this creative world of wish fulfillment, Ernest Worthing immediately arrives as a much more attractive alternative to political economy.

Like Gwendolen and Cecily, Miss Prism firmly takes the initiative in her sexual quest, advising Chasuble that "by persistently remaining single, a man converts himself into a permanent public temptation" (E50). When Chasuble enquires of Jack, "Your brother was, I believe, unmarried, was he not?" she remarks bitterly, "People who live entirely for pleasure usually are." She is prepared to wait in the church vestry for an hour and three quarters to waylay Chasuble, a rendezvous entirely of her own fabrication, and her decorous but relentless pursuit is crowned at the play's conclusion by a happy embrace and an enthusiastic "Frederick! At last!"

The two named manservants, reduced from the three of the four-act version by the exclusion of the gardener Moulton, function in counterpoint to their masters. The saturnine Lane, polished and ironic, seems derived from the Ideal Butler of *An Ideal Husband*, Phipps, whom Wilde described as follows: "He is a mask with a manner, of his intellectual or emotional life, history knows nothing. He represents the dominance of form" (W553). Lane's effortless intellectual supremacy to Algernon, expressed through his mastery of words, both establishes the prevailing verbal register and introduces the essentially amoral atmosphere. Algernon's observation, based on Lane's views on marriage, that the lower orders "have absolutely no sense of moral responsibility" is immediately confirmed by Jack's announcement that it is "pleasure, pleasure!" which brings him up to town: "What else should bring one anywhere?" The world of the play is a sybaritic one, shared by master and servant, enjoyed trivially by Algernon and more gravely by Lane, who well knows that in married households the champagne is rarely of a first-rate brand. Put on the spot by his master over the absence of the promised cucumber sandwiches, he rises effortlessly to the occasion with the urbane lie that there were no cucumbers in the market that morning, not even for ready money. To make the servant more elegant and poised than the master is part of Wilde's general strategy of inversion, just as the women are more powerful than the men. The more serious John Worthing has a servant whose name at least, Merriman, provides a contrast to him. Merriman's role is less prominent than Lane's. He is never called upon to do more than obey increasingly contradictory orders or announce visitors. Yet, even this apparently routine part makes a distinct contribution. Frank Dyall, who played Merriman on the opening night, recalled that his first lines—"Mr. Ernest Worthing has just driven over from the station. He has brought his luggage with him"—provided the loudest laugh he had ever experienced. When he came offstage, Wilde, who was backstage, said to him, "I am so glad you got that laugh. It shows they have followed the plot."[2]

The final character to be reckoned with, Lady Bracknell, is one of Wilde's most remarkable creations, with a formidable stage impact, indelibly imprinted on the collective theatrical memory by Edith Evans's interpretation, fortunately preserved in Asquith's film version. Lady Bracknell has antecedents in Wilde's earlier plays, notably the

Characters

Duchess of Berwick in *Lady Windermere's Fan,* who shares her ruthlessness, and Lady Hunstanton in *A Woman of No Importance,* who practices a similarly fractured, idiosyncratic logic. (In early drafts of *The Importance of Being Earnest,* Lady Bracknell is called Lady Brancaster: Hunstanton and Brancaster are neighboring villages in Norfolk.) Within the comedy's formal structure, she enacts the traditional obstructive role of the disapproving parent, initially disapproving of both betrothals. In fact, she assumes an authoritative position toward every character within the world of the play and, by natural extension, everyone outside it. As mother to Gwendolen, she is prepared to grant or withhold her disposal in marriage: "When you do become engaged to some one, I, or your father, should his health permit, will inform you of the fact. An engagement should come on a young girl as a surprise, pleasant or unpleasant, as the case may be. It is hardly a matter that she could be allowed to arrange for herself" (E26). There seems little likelihood of Lord Bracknell's health permitting any intervention. Lady Bracknell is equally prepared to act in loco parentis and give her consent to her nephew Algernon's engagement. She patronizes and interrogates Jack and Cecily, purchases Gwendolen's trusty maid's confidence by means of a small coin, snubs Canon Chasuble, and terrorizes Miss Prism. One of the most vivid shots in the Asquith film shows her perched on a pile of crates, as she rattles relentlessly in the luggage train on her mission to retrieve Gwendolen (whose own self-willed behavior offers a good imitation of her mother's).

Lady Bracknell thus provides the major source of conflict within the plot. She is the monster who has to be slain, or at least tamed, so that the conventions of comedy may triumph; she seems to stand for all that is most obstructive, conservative, and negative in Victorian society. But as the play unfolds, it becomes clear that she herself has manipulated life for years. She is as ready to change the fashionable side of Belgrave Square as she is to rearrange the seating plan of a dinner party, and she is quite prepared to enter Worthing's name on her list of eligible young men, should his answers to her questions be "what a really affectionate mother requires"; this list has the status of a specialized text, an equivalent to the girls' diaries and Miss Prism's novel. Her first question, somewhat disconcertingly, is "Do you smoke?" and the main thrust of her inquiry centers on Jack's income and property. Satisfied on that score, she then moves to "minor matters," and her question about Jack's family is interestingly phrased. It is not "Who are your parents?" (the more obvious form in view of Jack's comparative youth) but "Are your parents living?"—a matter likely to have a direct effect on Jack's wealth. Like the Duchess of Berwick in *Lady Windermere's Fan,* whose daughter Agatha becomes satisfactorily engaged to a rich young Australian, Lady Bracknell's prime concern is material. As she later comments in connection with Cecily's future, "When I married Lord Bracknell I had no fortune of any kind. But I never dreamed for a moment of allowing that to stand in my way." Significantly, her surreal advice to Jack is to "try and acquire some relatives as soon as possible, and to make a definite effort to produce at any rate one parent, of either sex, before the season is quite over" (E32). Parents, like property and government stocks, are essentially commodities, and marriage, an ordeal to be endured in order to secure wealth.

One of Lady Bracknell's most striking qualities is her unpredictability. After stating in an alarming preamble that "I have always been of opinion that a man who desires to get married should know either everything or nothing," she asks Jack, "Which do you know?" and the question comes like one of the Sphinx's riddles. Jack, after some understandable hesitation, replies, "I know nothing, Lady Bracknell," and waits for his doom to be pronounced. Her reaction is instructive: "I am pleased to hear it. I do not approve of anything that tampers with natural ignorance. Ignorance is like a delicate exotic fruit; touch it and the bloom is gone. The whole theory of modern education is radically unsound. Fortunately in England, at any rate, education produces no effect whatsoever. If it did, it would prove a serious danger to the upper classes, and probably lead to acts of violence in Grosvenor Square. What is your income?" (E27).

To begin with, the wish to marry her daughter to someone who knows nothing is startling. But in this imagined, idealized world of aristocratic ease, a member of the upper classes will not be expected to earn a living; and, in any event, as has been established, he will have smoking, that prime example of conspicuous consumption, as an occupation. Besides, a man in the full bloom of natural ignorance is much more easily manipulated by a woman and is therefore much more interesting. (As Gwendolen later confesses to Jack, "The simplicity of your character makes you exquisitely incomprehensible to me.") Lady Bracknell then delivers one of those statements which link the play, finely but most effectively, with the real world and remind us that Wilde was also the author of *The Soul of Man under Socialism.* Lady Bracknell speaks with irrefutable logic: if the middle or lower classes were properly educated, the upper classes could not continue their privileged life of pleasure for a moment. This merest hint of underlying instability, picked up by later references to the French Revolution or to the notion that the exploded Bunbury might have been the victim of a revolutionary outrage, anchors the play's surreal world to a society in which unwanted babies actually were regularly abandoned at railway stations. It also serves to authenticate Lady Bracknell's peculiar brand of benevolent tyranny. The surreal power of the role makes it suitable for cross-casting, notably William Hutt's performance in a Stratford (Ontario) Festival production in 1976 at the Avon Theater. There is some method in her apparent eccentricity, and her flights of verbal exuberance lift her to the level of genuine creativity. Supremely, she is able to mold the world to her desire; and although in families of high position "strange coincidences are not supposed to occur," it is entirely appropriate that Lady Bracknell initiates the play's resolution by telling Jack who he really is.

8

Structure and Style

The style in which *The Importance of Being Earnest* is acted is crucial. Wilde, in spite of the reactions of contemporary critics, with their references to W. S. Gilbert, was not imitating standard British farce, in which sheer pace and physicality were major ingredients and in which the performers tended to signal the verbal jokes. Wilde's own stage directions, the comments of perceptive critics, and the experience of actors and actresses over the years agree on one simple principle: that the play's wit is most effective when the performers are seriously absorbed in their roles and give no indication that anything is being done or said for comic impact. The actors in the original production were aware that Wilde's text was indefinably different from the norm, and they were themselves drawn from George Alexander's selected company at the St. James's Theatre, which specialized in elegant and sophisticated society plays. Dyall, the original Merriman, who remembered Wilde's "delicious enjoyment" at the first cast reading, also recalled the actors' judgment on that occasion, that only they would appreciate it and that it would not get over to the public. Irene Vanbrugh, cast as Gwendolen, found the style of writing entirely different from that of anything she had ever appeared in and very difficult to come to terms with; only when she had learnt to speak it "as though coming from myself" could she relax and begin to enjoy the wit.[1]

One key to the correct style is concerned with pace. In George Alexander and Allan Aynesworth, the first Jack and the first Algernon, Wilde was fortunate in securing highly accomplished and controlled actors, who would not strain for cheap comic effect. Even so, Max Beerbohm, commenting on the 1902 revival, criticized Alexander, who should have known better, for "bustling in at break-neck speed" in the famous "mourning" entrance in Act Two when the situation demanded the "slowest of entries."[2] John Gielgud, a consummate actor and director of Wilde, commented that he realized only toward the end of his career that the muffin-eating sequence at the close of Act Two was more effective if played slowly, "with real solemnity." His phrase should be read by every actor or director before beginning work on a production of *The Importance of Being Earnest:* "You must not indulge yourself, or caricature."[3]

The play, of course, like a complex piece of music, which it resembles, is not written in one tempo. There are many sequences that call for swift speech or action, and Wilde often indicates these, as when Algernon dictates his profession of love to Cecily "speaking very rapidly": "Cecily, ever since I first looked upon your wonderful and incomparable beauty, I have dared to love you wildly, passionately, devotedly, hopelessly" (E61). The speed is partly to overcome Algernon's embarrassment and partly to eliminate the preliminary nervous cough, "Ahem! Ahem!" which Cecily does not know how to spell. It is also absurd in its reversal of the usual practice of slowing down for dictation and in its transformation of what should be a private, heartfelt, spontaneous declaration of love into a sequence that will look good in a diary meant for publication. Having set up the joke, Wilde immediately counters it, first with Cecily's interruption as she seizes on and objects to "hopelessly" and then with Merriman's announcement, "The dog-cart is waiting, sir," which serves to underline the hopelessness of the situation and slows the pace right down again.

The variety of pace, as well as Wilde's subtle orchestration of it, permeates a text that has begun with the sound of Algernon playing the piano. There are even sections that are arranged as duets, as when Gwendolen "beats time with uplifted finger" for "Your Christian names are still an insuperable barrier. That is all!" To this, Jack and Algernon reply by speaking together. That sequence at the opening of Act Three continues with perfect symmetry until the double embrace is brought to a shocked conclusion by Merriman's tactful cough and the bombshell of his announcement: "Lady Bracknell."

In contrast to the text of *An Ideal Husband,* which contains full and detailed stage directions, the published text of *The Importance of Being Earnest* is more reticent, and Wilde seems to have toned down some aspects of the physical side of Alexander's production in revising the play for publication. (It came out in February 1899, and Wilde, exiled in France, was dependent on materials sent to him from Alexander by his publisher, Smithers.) That refinement was part of the process initiated when, at Alexander's earlier request, he compressed the looser, more indulgent four-act version into three acts. In the four-act version, all the characters were provided with different books during the frantic hunt for General Moncrieff's Christian name: Chasuble has a railway guide; Cecily, a *History of Our Own Times;* Miss Prism, pricelists from the Civil Service Stores; and Lady Bracknell, a copy of Robert Hichens's novel *The Green Carnation* (published in September 1894, this contained thinly disguised portraits of Wilde and Douglas as Mr. Amarinth and Lord Reggie). In the three-act version, Wilde has reduced this self-indulgent joke to the only relevant reference book, the Army Lists. In the original production, however, the reviewer of the *Referee* recorded that the whole company was "provided with copies of the Army List, everyone searching for the name of the foundling."[4] Wilde's considered stage direction makes it clear that Jack alone conducts the search: first he rushes to the bookcase to tear the books out, and then, when he has located his father's Christian names, Ernest John, he "puts book very quietly down and speaks quite calmly." The mass comic scene, potentially frenetic, is replaced by a much more concentrated burst of energy, which is then transformed into a moment of stillness, with the focus sharply on Jack. Wilde, like a conductor, brings in and integrates each instrument with total control and is especially skillful in knowing how long any one solo or section should continue. Much of the play's special quality is contained in the tension between action and style, between the absurdity of what a character does (hunting for his father's Christian names in a reference work, dictating a declaration of love) and the elegance or aplomb with which it is carried out or commented upon.

Style, visually conveyed by the immaculate dress and surface manners of each character, from Lady Bracknell to the servants, is most distinctively and consistently expressed through the language. Some early critics complained that all the characters talked in the same voice. They all, in fact, with minor exceptions, tended to talk like Wilde. As the critic of the *Graphic* conceded, the same indictment was brought against Sheridan.[5] Wilde attempted to answer that criticism, which had been made about *An Ideal Husband,* in his interview with Ross in the *St. James's Gazette:*

> "Have you heard it said that all the characters in your play talk as you do?"
>
> "Rumours of that kind have reached me from time to time," said Mr. Wilde, lighting a cigarette, "and I should fancy that some such criticism has been made. The fact is that it is only in the last few years that the dramatic critic has had the opportunity of seeing plays written by anyone who has a mastery of style. In the case of a dramatist also an artist it is impossible not to feel that the work of art, to be a work of art, must be dominated by the artist. Every play of Shakespeare is dominated by Shakespeare. Ibsen and Dumas dominate their works. My works are dominated by myself."[6]

Certainly, all the characters in *The Importance of Being Earnest* talk in a highly self-conscious way. Almost every speech seems to be made for effect, rather than to give an impression of spontaneity; perhaps, it would be more accurate to say that every character appears to speak spontaneously in language that requires an audience. Just as Gwendolen and Cecily expect to be, and exist to be, looked at, so they and the other characters speak to be listened to. Gwendolen's two opening speeches define the manner:

ALGERNON (to GWENDOLEN): Dear me, you are smart!

GWENDOLEN: I am always smart! Am I not, Mr. Worthing?

JACK: You're quite perfect, Miss Fairfax.

GWENDOLEN: Oh! I hope I am not that. It would leave no
room for developments, and I intend to develop in many directions. (E18)

To her cousin's comment, Gwendolen offers both a correction and a
significant self-definition, immediately counteracting any misconceived
notion that she is a conventionally modest young woman. She then
takes the sexual initiative by turning to Jack and deliberately including
him in the conversation, in defiance of social etiquette and in her
mother's presence. The formally accurate "Am I not?" rather than the
colloquial "Aren't I?" draws attention to the precision of her speech
and action. To Jack's compliment, she again offers a qualification,
which for a brief moment sounds conventionally deprecating, but is
subtly transformed into a self-recognition of her high potential and
ambition. The final enigmatic phrase, "and I intend to develop in many
directions," expresses both a sense of her formidable will, and her
instinctive ability to construct and shape an apparently polite phrase to
achieve maximum impact. It suggests everything and yet sounds sufficiently like the well-tutored piety of a respectable Victorian girl to be
uttered in front of her mother. It is crystal clear that when mentioning
"development," Gwendolen does not have the University Extension
Scheme in mind.

Gwendolen is, undoubtedly, always smart. Cecily, though differ-
entiated from Gwendolen by a greater simplicity of expression, shares
the same heightened self-awareness. Her first speech, as with
Gwendolen's, reveals her acute interest in her own image: "I know
perfectly well that I look quite plain after my German lesson" (E41).
When Algernon introduces himself with "You are my little cousin
Cecily, I'm sure," she swiftly contradicts him: "You are under some
strange mistake. I am not little. In fact I believe I am more than usual-

ly tall for my age." The unexpected fullness of that "under some strange mistake" suggests a pleasure in language and a command of words that begins to establish her as autonomous, an impression consolidated by her correction of Algernon and soon confirmed by her full and authoritative reply to his denial "You mustn't think that I am wicked": "If you are not, then you have certainly been deceiving us all in a very inexcusable manner. I hope you have not been leading a double life, pretending to be wicked and being really good all the time. That would be hypocrisy" (E46). Algernon may well look at Cecily "in amazement" as she contradicts every presumption that she is the naive and innocent ingenue that she appears to be by her dress, her age, and her situation. When he attempts to adjust his image to something more acceptable, saying, "Oh! Of course I have been rather reckless," her reply, "I am glad to hear it," is identical to one of Lady Bracknell's comments to Jack, thereby returning the audience to an appreciation of the underlying unity of the text.

When Gwendolen and Cecily rise and confront each other over the teacups, they play variations within a register and rhythmic pattern that Wilde has developed from the play's opening exchanges:

> GWENDOLEN: From the moment I saw you I distrusted you. I felt that you were false and deceitful. I am never deceived in such matters. My first impressions of people are invariably right.

> CECILY: It seems to me, Miss Fairfax, that I am trespassing on your valuable time. No doubt you have many other calls of a similar character to make in the neighbourhood. (E73)

Wilde is so much in command of the play's rhythm that he is able to move from that elegant hostility to the equally balanced and equally well constructed affection of "My poor wounded Cecily!" and "My sweet wronged Gwendolen!" within a page, or about two minutes of stage time. Again Wilde's minute attention to the play's mood is noticeable in the stage direction that accompanies Gwendolen's "You will call me sister, will you not?": *(slowly and seriously)* (E75). The line itself comes from melodrama or from a sentimental three-volume novel, but must be delivered with the appearance of utter sincerity, thus drawing attention to its double artificiality. The play as a whole, as Wilde told Ada Leverson, should go like a pistol shot; but it should always maintain strict decorum and never slide into vulgar exaggeration or convey an impression of haste.

It is possible to identify three main strands of language within the remarkably homogeneous text: that of the four lovers, witty, elegant, polished, self-possessed; that of Lady Bracknell, who erupts into the play with a deployment of words as original and disconcerting as her attitudes; and the overlapping but still distinct register of Canon Chasuble and Miss Prism, with its mixture of pedantic precept and idiosyncratic diversion. Lady Bracknell's style of speech has an extraordinary quality of unpredictability, which stems partly from the shape of her sentences and partly from the sequence of her thoughts and logic. The description of tea with Lady Harbury provides an early example of her manner: "I'm sorry if we are a little late, Algernon, but I was obliged to call on dear Lady Harbury. I hadn't been there since her poor husband's death. I never saw a woman so altered; she looks quite twenty years younger" (E19). The "obliged" strikes the first note of reservation: the visit was a social obligation, rather than an act of kindness. The "dear Lady Harbury" and "her poor husband's death" build toward the "alteration" with the expectation of Lady Bracknell's sympathy, only to be shattered by the "twenty years younger" and the request for a cup of tea. The cucumber story follows, to which Lady Bracknell replies, "It really makes no matter, Algernon. I had some crumpets with Lady Harbury, who seems to me to be living entirely for pleasure now." Those "crumpets" and the rebuke about living entirely for pleasure seem to turn the eating of crumpets into the equivalent of sexual indulgence: a woman who can serve crumpets might be capable of anything; and the word *pleasure* echoes Jack's original statement as to what has brought him up to town. Algernon then makes a smart comment (borrowed from *The Picture of Dorian Gray*): "I hear her hair has turned quite gold from grief," which is a good example of the contrasting "witty" register. Lady Bracknell's response is less expected: "It certainly has changed its colour. From what cause I, of course, cannot say." There can be only one explanation for Lady Harbury's sudden return to youth, and Lady Bracknell knows it. But her redundant "of course" marks her social refusal to go on public record as endorsing such a vulgar suggestion, serves to emphasize her knowledge of the explanation, and yet disconcertingly manages to suggest some alternative and even more scandalous cause. These additions and interjections, which seem to follow the unusual swoops and contours of Lady Bracknell's mind, come into their own in the famous handbag passage, in which her persistent refusal to express the slightest touch of sympathy at Jack's revelation that he is an orphan provides the concealed edge to her convoluted response: "To be born, or at any rate bred, in a hand-bag, whether it had handles or not, seems to me to display a contempt for the ordinary decencies of family life that reminds one of the worst excesses of the French Revolution. And I presume you know what that unfortunate movement led to?" (E32). The judgment, after a number of diversions—"or at any rate bred," "whether it had handles or not"—is absolute, if absurd. The incident is symptomatic of chaos. Lady Harbury's crumpets indicated sexual immorality; for someone with the appearance of a gentleman, possessing town and country houses, 1,500 acres and an income of between £7,000 and £8,000 a year in investments, to be bred in a handbag and to be asking for the hand of the Honorable Gwendolen Fairfax signals revolution. Lady Bracknell's language rises superbly to the occasion, with an unsettling mixture of the pedantically accurate and the surreal: "I would strongly advise you, Mr. Worthing, to try and acquire some relations as soon as possible, and to make a definite effort to produce at any rate one parent, of either sex, before the season is quite over." Here "definite" and the surprising concessions represented by "at any rate" and "of either sex" reflect the individuality of Lady Bracknell, while the injunction to set the time scale to coincide with the social season makes a wonderfully absurd conclusion to her impossible conditions.

The third register, that of Chasuble and Prism, probes the phrases and rhythms of standard Victorian earnestness and morality. They share with Lady Bracknell the impulse to develop an idea to its fullest extent. For example, their reaction to Jack's arrival in mourning offers an extravagant verbal decoration around the central image:

CHASUBLE: Dear Mr. Worthing, I trust this garb of woe does not betoken some terrible calamity?

JACK: My brother.

MISS PRISM: More shameful debts and extravagance?

CHASUBLE: Still leading his life of pleasure?

JACK (shaking his head): Dead!

CHASUBLE: Your brother Ernest dead?

MISS PRISM: What a lesson for him! I trust he will profit by it. (E51)

Chasuble's orotund "garb of woe" and the tortuous syntax of his negative question, together with his apparent inability to comprehend Jack's quite explicit announcement, mocks the pedantic rhetoric of the clergy but also turns it into an art form. Miss Prism, in contrast to Chasuble but rather like Lady Bracknell in the latter's reaction to Bunbury's demise, shows an unnerving single-mindedness in her delivery of a moral judgment. When Jack reveals that Ernest has succumbed to a severe chill, she comments, "As a man sows, so shall he reap," yet one more moral precept, this time with biblical authority behind it but also one with a bizarre logic, indicating that the chill might have been caused by an absence of clothes or reprehensible night excursions. Yet, Wilde, while using the couple as a kind of choric commentary, also skillfully differentiates them, to highlight the sexual tension that hovers around their relationship. Thus, when Chasuble offers conventional spiritual support in saying, "What seem to us bitter trials are often blessings in disguise," Prism counters, "This seems to me a blessing of an extremely obvious kind." When Algy appears, resurrecting Ernest, and Cecily effects the reconciliation with Jack, Chasuble's commendation "You have done a beautiful action today, dear child" is neatly qualified by Prism's sententious "We must not be premature in our judgments" (E57).

There is no character and almost no part of the dialogue (with the exception of a few rather lame and standard jokes, such as the dentist/false impression exchange) that does not contribute to the overall sense of a text as intricate and controlled as a musical score. Every line requires attention to shape and rhythm, requires to be delivered rather than merely spoken. Max Beerbohm, reviewing the 1902 revival by George Alexander, made an attempt to define the kind of acting that the style of the play—and above all the nature of its language—demands:

> Before we try to define how it should be acted, let us try to define its character. In scheme, of course, it is a hackneyed farce—the story of a young man coming up to London "on the spree," and of another young man going down conversely to the country, and of the complications that ensue. In treatment, also, it is farcical, in so far as some of the fun depends on absurd "situations," "stage-business," and so forth. Thus one might assume that the best way to act it would be to rattle through it. That were a gross error. For, despite the scheme of the play, the fun depends mainly on what the characters say, rather than what they do. . . . What differentiates this farce from any other, and makes it funnier than any other, is the humorous contrast between its style and matter. To preserve its style fully, the dialogue must be spoken with grave unction. The sound and the sense of the words must be taken seriously, treated beautifully.

Beerbohm criticized the cast at the St. James's Theatre, which included Alexander himself as Jack, for rattling through the play; the only exception was Lilian Braithwaite, who acted the part of Cecily Cardew in precisely the right key of grace and dignity and, in seeming to take her part quite seriously, showed that she realized the full extent of its fun.[7]

Beerbohm's strictures on Alexander indicate the difficulty the play presents. It needs to be acted seriously but lightly, not hurriedly but not heavily. The actor and director who embodied the "Wildean" style in the 1930s and 1940s was John Gielgud, whose elegance and precision, both in gesture and speech, epitomized the "high" style of

English theater. Gielgud presided over strongly cast productions, in glittering settings and costumes by Cecil Beaton or Rex Whistler, that celebrated the polished comic patterns of an age to which the theater-going public looked back with nostalgia. Anthony Asquith's 1952 film encapsulates many of the glories of this style and period, incorporating brilliant performances from, for instance, two actresses who had stamped themselves on their roles, Edith Evans as Lady Bracknell and Margaret Rutherford as Miss Prism. But almost every member of the cast, which included Michael Redgrave as Jack, Michael Denison as Algy, Miles Malleson as Canon Chasuble, Joan Greenwood as Gwendolen, and Dorothy Tutin as Cecily, may be taken as excellent examples of the theatrical approach to Wilde of the period: they were professional Wildeans. The film is closely based on stage tradition; indeed, it begins, like Olivier's film *Henry V,* in a theater, with members of the audience in full evening dress sitting down in a private box and viewing the stage through a pair of opera glasses; and although there are scenes in Jack's rooms in the Albany and brief outdoor locations (such as Lady Bracknell's train journey to Hertfordshire) that are not in the play itself, the film remains unashamedly theatrical. A whole tradition of English acting, especially as represented in Gielgud's outstanding 1942 production, is preserved in this film.

Since the 1980s, directors have begun to cut through the cocoon of "classical" English acting and opulent design, in which Wilde's play was in danger of becoming smothered, and uncovered something sharper and more astringent. Peter Hall's production for the English National Theatre in 1982 contained a memorable performance by Judi Dench as an unusually youthful-looking Lady Bracknell; it also offered an exceptionally lucid reading of the play, in which the musical construction and rhythm were always apparent and yet which managed to hint both at a subtext of emotion and to convey the thrust of Eric Bentley's insight that "what begins as a prank ends as a criticism of life. What begins as intellectual high-kicking ends as intellectual sharpshooting."[8] Michael Billington, reviewing the production in the *Guardian,* commented, "The people themselves are motivated by recognisable passions like lust and greed; yet the world they inhabit, half-way between W. S. Gilbert and Alice in Wonderland, exists at a slight tangent to normality." The play's strange, topsy-turvy quality was hinted at in John Bury's designs: "The second-act garden, for instance, has a glassy, reflecting surface, sporadic rose-trees (again a hint of Alice?) and a silhouetted village background. Visually, the production makes the point that Wilde transports us into a timeless, Victorian fairy-land. But, textually, it never lets us forget that Wilde also offers us a daisy-chain of serious comment on death, marriage, morals, the class-system, the decline of aristocracy."[9] Hall's production restored the sense of edge, of danger, in Wilde's farce, reminding its audiences that the double standard, the central joke around which the play is constructed, was, and is, at the core of English life and society.

The design by Bob Crowley for Nicholas Hytner's 1993 production at the Aldwych Theatre announced that this reading of the text was verging on the postmodern. Everything was slightly larger than life and set at a slight angle. An elongated scarlet sofa dominated Algy's red-and-green rooms in Half-Moon Street, and a vast reproduction of Sargent's portrait of W. Graham Robertson stared out at the audience. As John Stokes remarked, it hinted at "a taste in domestic furnishing that might reflect a lurid private life."[10] When the action moved to rural Hertfordshire, Crowley conceived a visual rejection of the conventional English country garden: "a brutally geometric topiary hedge, tall enough at one end to accommodate a giant porthole affording a perspective view of the manor house overlooking the parterre and central allée of a Le Nôtre garden, and sloping across the full width of the stage"—the hedge was in the shape of a peacock in colors that echoed the red and green of Mayfair, underlining the artificiality of this decadent escape to nature and the essentially urban thrust of the play's dynamics. Although some critics accused Maggie Smith of upsetting the play's balance by a too relentless pursuit of comic effects, her performance had a terrifying, predatory dimension. Irving Wardle described her as a plumed, steel-gray vulture, "part suburban *parvenu,* part drag artist, part vigilantly suspicious rodent."[11] In the cruelty and intensity of her desires, she resembled a character from a Ben Jonson play, perhaps from *Volpone*. In John Peter's summary for the *Sunday Times,* the play is more than just fireworks: "It is a social and aesthetic chess game in which sincerity is ranged against style. Style wins over sincerity because Wilde despaired of finding any of the latter. In one sense this play, like all great comedies, is about nothing in particular: it exists to justify its own existence. But behind the wit and the ostentatious elegance of the writing, you get a glimpse of a barren, glittering desert."[12]

It is significant that the reviewers took the opportunity of this major Wilde revival in London to attempt to redefine and revalue so well known a play. The director, too, had clearly been studying recent Wilde criticism; the possible sexual ambivalence that hovers around the name Ernest was hinted at more than once. What the production demonstrated, above all, was the crucial role of style within the play, style that needs to be conveyed consistently through decor, costumes, gesture, and speech, in this most unforgiving but also most rewarding of theatrical texts.

9

Flux

The world that the characters of *The Importance of Being Earnest* inhabit is a mixture of the reassuringly stable and the chaotically surreal. Society, led by its spokesperson Lady Bracknell, offers the appearance of respectability, but the respectable has a disconcerting habit of vanishing, like the body of Lewis Carroll's Cheshire Cat, leaving only a grin behind, a mocking trace of what was present moments before. Nothing, and no one, can be relied on absolutely. As Lady Bracknell comments grimly when Jack offers the Court Guides of the period as proof of the late Thomas Cardew's three addresses, "I have known strange errors in that publication" (E89).

The individual characters are capable of rapid transformations. Miss Prism is a case in point. Lady Bracknell inquires, "Is this Miss Prism a female of repellent aspect, remotely connected with education?" Canon Chasuble replies indignantly, "She is the most cultivated of ladies, and the very picture of respectability." Lady Bracknell observes icily, "It is obviously the same person" (E97). Cecily and Gwendolen move from professions of friendship to blatant hostility and back again to sisterhood in the space of a few minutes. Jack arrives at his home in deep mourning for his fictional younger brother Ernest, only to make a fast and smooth adjustment on finding him apparently alive and well. Miss Prism, temporarily the guardian of propriety, draws attention to this disturbing state of flux: "After we had all been resigned to his loss, his sudden return seems to me peculiarly distressing" (E55).

Another aspect of uncertainty is the play's family structure, or rather lack of it. Only Gwendolen of the four lovers is in a position to produce both parents, and by all accounts, Lord Bracknell plays a minimal part in her life. Cecily has, it seems, no parents at all and is described simply as the granddaughter of the late Thomas Cardew, as much an orphan as her guardian Jack: old Mr. Cardew is a kind of universal fairy godfather, a benevolent deus ex machina traveling the nation's railways like the kind old gentleman in Mrs. Nesbitt's *The Railway Children*. Jack has lost both his parents and is a foundling. Algernon knows who his parents were, but never refers to them and cannot recall his father's Christian name because they were "never even on speaking terms." The fact that General Moncrieff died before Algernon was a year old makes the logic watertight, but the implication that there are a great many families in which fathers and sons do not communicate runs deeper. Lady Bracknell, presumably acting in loco parentis for her poor sister Mrs. Moncrieff and the first absent and then deceased general, entrusts her charge to a governess. This, of course, would be "normal" practice in a Victorian upper-class family. Equally normally, if more understandably, Cecily's education is placed in the hands of Miss Prism, a benevolent, if potentially wayward, influence, as it transpires. The sinister potential of young orphans, a disengaged guardian, a secluded country house, and a governess would be explored by Henry James in his chilling echo of Wilde's play, *The Turn of the Screw*. Wilde offered to a Victorian society that prided itself on family values and stability an image of a highly volatile collection of individuals. Lady Bracknell's role can be viewed, in part, as the measured attempts of the matriarch to impose some kind of acceptable order on a society intent on dissolving before her eyes. When, on her visit to the Manor House, she hears of the "death" of Bunbury, it seems for a moment that chaos is receding; a certain death is infinitely preferable to the previous state of uncertainty. She then learns that

Cecily and Algernon are engaged to be married. "I do not know," she comments *"with a shiver,"* "whether there is anything peculiarly exciting in the air of this particular part of Hertfordshire, but the number of engagements that go on seems to me considerably above the proper average that statistics have laid down for our guidance" (E88). That shiver expresses perfectly her own and her social class's innate distrust of change.

Family bonds, one of the staples of social (and comic) structure, turn out to be minimal. The apparently rigid, accepted framework of relationships and social conventions can be circumvented, and the young people, indeed all the characters, are potentially free to pursue their instincts and the prompting of their imaginations. In a Shakespearean romantic comedy, such as *A Midsummer Night's Dream* or *As You Like It,* the characters would need to enter the moonlit wood or the forest of Arden to approach the threshold of release and, as a second stage in their initiation, be subject to the juice of Oberon's magical flower or undergo the metamorphosis of disguise and gender exchange. Wilde's characters achieve a double life with no drastic change of milieu or appearance. A train ticket to London and an engraved card transform Jack into Ernest; by putting on a country suit and inventing a telegram Algernon can escape from his aunt's dinner party to attend the nonexistent Bunbury's bedside. Cecily's and Gwendolen's diaries merely record the adventures organized by their active imaginations. The fictional "as if" existence overlays the objective, mundane world, which looks so familiar. The characters, cut free from traditional family ties, the most restrictive that can be conceived, are released to create a much more interesting life, designing it effortlessly to their own specifications.

Lewis Carroll's landscape offers some interesting analogies to Wilde's, though Alice enters Wonderland through a conventional device, the tunnel that turns into a shaft down which she hurtles in free-fall. Carroll's pattern of action is, on the surface, rather more robust than Wilde's, closer, in fact, to the prevailing tone of late Victorian farce. Carroll introduces motifs that seem like uncanny anticipations of Wilde. The Duchess, for example, offers a complete reversal of the standard Victorian myth of affection toward young children. The setting for this piece of child abuse is a nightmarish Victorian kitchen whose air is thick with pepper and flying saucepans, inhabited by a raging cook:

> Speak roughly to your little boy,
> And beat him when he sneezes:
> He only does it to annoy,
> Because he knows it teases.

The Duchess then flings the baby at Alice and leaves to get ready to play croquet with the Queen. The baby snorts like a steam engine. Alice ties it up into a knot, only to find that it is beginning to turn into a pig, and she is quite relieved when it trots off quietly into the wood and is never seen again. Jack, likewise entrusted to an unmotherly female, is also roughly handled. Wheeled through the smoky London streets to a noisy railway station, he is treated like a parcel and abandoned in the left-luggage office, to be replaced in his bassinet by the manuscript of a three-volume novel. Unlike the pig-baby, he returns.

In the structure of the Alice books, dream time is set against a framework of waking reality. In most stage comedies, the plot is resolved after some transforming experience or an admission of guilt or error. Wilde, in *The Importance of Being Earnest,* employs none of these generally reassuring processes. As has been argued, the fictional, creative double life, the life of will, instinct, appetite, egotism, permeates the conventional world of social "reality." At the play's conclusion, this fictional life turns out to be not only more powerful and attractive but, slightly alarmingly, truthful as well. Moreover, this double life is not morally superior to social reality. It offers no psychological depth or imaginative insight, no magical dream experience or allegorical test of character. It is simply far more satisfactory, in that it provides satisfaction, unlike the sterile mechanisms of Albee's *The American Dream.* In *The Importance of Being Earnest* the characters manipulate the rules and triumphantly achieve what they want.

The subplot of Prism and Chasuble echoes this central principle, which is especially clear in the development of the two betrothals.

Each is relatively advanced in years, and each is condemned by society to celibacy, as ritual guardians of education, which obviously includes moral education and religion. Miss Prism even lectures the poorer classes of the parish on the necessity for "thrift," by which, in practical terms, she presumably means a choice between birth control or sexual abstinence. In the four-act version, both Chasuble and Prism had longer roles, and Chasuble had several opportunities to expand his views on celibacy. In the three-act text, Wilde made him deliver them with superb economy: "The precept as well as the practice of the Primitive Church was distinctly against matrimony." But even as Chasuble speaks, he betrays his realization, conscious or unconscious, that precept and practice do not necessarily coincide, and so proclaims himself a potential convert to the new morality. As Miss Prism comments, "That is obviously the reason why the Primitive Church has not lasted up to the present day" (E50). In the post-Darwinian age, sexual selection rules. Miss Prism, who in the first scenario even harbored matrimonial designs on her employer, clearly has her sights fixed on the rector and conducts an elaborate courtship game into which Chasuble is perfectly willing to be drawn. Apparently condemned by their occupations and comic names to a subsidiary role, they are used by Wilde in a much more flexible way, becoming from time to time the mouthpiece for some of his funniest and most incisive comments. For example, within their verbal maneuvers on the subject of marriage, they deliver these resonant judgments:

MISS PRISM: No married man is ever attractive except to his wife.

CHASUBLE: And often, I've been told, not even to her. (E50)

The statements work in two ways. They indicate, perhaps, at a primary level, a comic fear of sex and intimacy. They are simultaneously a resigned acknowledgment of the deadening effect of marriage on sexual attraction. On the lips of younger or more sophisticated characters, on Gwendolen's or Algernon's, the implications would be less startling. When these epitomes of respectability pronounce such clear-eyed verdicts, the conventional myths begin to appear frayed and insubstantial.

The state of marriage is defined as very far from ideal, even demoralizing, an inescapable fact established both explicitly and implicitly throughout the play. In married households, as Lane observes, the champagne is rarely of a first-rate brand. General Moncrieff was essentially a man of peace, except in his domestic life. Lord Bracknell dines upstairs and is perhaps a fictional invalid, even a polite fiction, like Bunbury. Lady Harbury looks twenty years younger since her husband's death. After three weeks with a "thoroughly experienced French maid," Lady Lancing's own husband did not know her, while according to Algernon, after six months nobody knew her (E90). The possible sexual connotations of the French maid's experience and the different meanings of the word *know* provide incidental levels of ambiguity. The cumulative effect of all these references is to explode the myth of the stability of marriage. Yet, that is the very destiny of six of the characters in the play, a destiny that, perversely, they seem willing to embrace just as eagerly as they embrace each other. They do it in the clear knowledge that the tableau with which the play ends is a convenient, palpable, and even temporary artifice. Perhaps the most subversive comment within the highly structured, operatic finale is Gwendolen's reply to Jack's confession:

> JACK: Gwendolen, it is a terrible thing for a man to find out suddenly that all his life he has been speaking nothing but the truth. Can you forgive me?

> GWENDOLEN: I can. For I feel that you are sure to change. (E104)

This is the Gwendolen who has just declared, "I never change, except in my affections," a declaration that Cecily has ringingly endorsed: "What a noble nature you have, Gwendolen!" Just so Jack, recognizing the true, dandiacal, egotistical insight of Gwendolen, eagerly accepts her philosophy of serious triviality: "My own one!"

The traditional form of comedy indicates that some kind of new experience or insight, some liberating ritual, will accompany the shift toward harmony and reconciliation. In *The Importance of Being Earnest* the promised ritual is the projected christening, in which the "adult" males will be reborn to their lovers' specifications. The intention is signaled by an elaborate quasi-musical sequence:

GWENDOLEN and CECILY *(speaking together):* Your Christian names are still an insuperable barrier. That is all!

JACK and ALGERNON *(speaking together):* Our Christian names! Is that all? But we are going to be christened this afternoon.

GWENDOLEN *(to JACK):* For my sake you are prepared to do this terrible thing?

JACK: I am.

CECILY *(to ALGERNON):* To please me you are ready to face this fearful ordeal?

ALGERNON: I am!

GWENDOLEN: How absurd to talk of the equality of the sexes! Where questions of self-sacrifice are concerned, men are infinitely beyond us.

JACK: We are. *(Clasps hands with ALGERNON.)*

CECILY: They have moments of physical courage of which we women know absolutely nothing.

GWENDOLEN *(to JACK):* Darling!

ALGERNON *(to CECILY):* Darling! *(They fall into each other's arms.)* (E85–86)

The "speaking together" highlights the sense of interchangeability between the couples. In spite of the external, conventional differences (Jack older, more serious, "Ernest" in town: Algy younger, flippant, "Bunburying" in the country), the men are as one in the "essentials" and clasp hands to cement their union. Gwendolen, urbane and sophisiticated, finds her perfect complement in Cecily's self-taught singleness of purpose. The unison speaking and the mirrored gestures draw attention to the contrived solution and so to the implied contrivance of all such acts of "courage." The great emotional moment, when lovers fall into each other's arms, is exposed as purely gestural, dependent on the absurd test of a hastily arranged christening. It is also, of course, ephemeral, since Wilde has built the sequence step-by-step until it must be exploded by Merriman's announcement of Lady Bracknell's arrival. The double christening, too, is only a gesture: it never occurs and is replaced by the revelation of the slightly ominous truth that Jack is "naturally" Ernest, having been named after his father: the example of General Moncrieff's married life is unlikely to reassure.

But marriage, in this ferocious idyll, is a distinctly alarming state. Canon Chasuble's pronouncement that "the precept as well as the practice of the Primitive Church was distinctly against matrimony" has much to commend it, even if he ultimately abandons his long-held beliefs. Algy strikes the first note of warning in Act One: "Nothing will induce me to part with Bunbury, and if you ever get married, which seems to me extremely problematic, you will be very glad to know Bunbury. A man who marries without knowing Bunbury has a very tedious time of it." Gwendolen's are perhaps the most revealing insights into the nature of marriage. Before Jack's proposal, she expresses pity for any woman who is married to a man called John: "She would probably never be allowed to know the entrancing pleasure of a single moment's solitude." Later, after the revelations about Jack's origins, she gives her views on marriage as an institution: "Whatever influence I ever had over mamma, I lost at the age of three. But although she may prevent us from becoming man and wife, and I may marry someone else, and marry often, nothing that she can possibly do can alter my eternal devotion to you." That "marry often" is the kind of surreal elaboration within the text that undercuts the achieved symmetry of the close, emphasizing it as something purely artistic and implying that the institution itself, reflected in the final tableau, is mere convention, pure formality. The pattern pleases, but it is purely pattern, purely form, subject to artistic license and, thus, to change. The characters do not need to return from one world to another, to come back from the disquieting dream or Wonderland into which they have penetrated: they have been creating it all the time.

As Miss Prism says of her three-volume novel, "The good ended happily, and the bad unhappily. That is what Fiction means." Wilde's characters are all scriptwriters and storytellers: Chasuble's adaptable sermons, Prism's novel, Cecily's and Gwendolen's diaries, Lady Bracknell's list of eligible young men. Jack and Algy invent characters, a wicked younger brother and the invalid Bunbury, to enable them to escape from the restrictions of Victorian life and morality. Jack retreats from the responsibilities of his country life—as guardian to Cecily, local landowner, justice of the peace—to go to London, ostensibly to sort out the dreadful scrapes his brother gets into. Once in London, he actually becomes Ernest, presumably spending a good proportion of his time in the company of the extravagant but penniless Algy. Algy, meanwhile, flits from a London life where he is at the beck and call of his Aunt Augusta to the country, Bunburying all over Shropshire on two separate occasions. The dual fictions allow each bachelor to live a double life. The young women, in contrast, cannot wait to be married so that their double life can begin. Gwendolen, as she admits, may marry someone else if she is prevented from achieving Ernest and may marry often. Algy says he could wait for Cecily until she was thirty-five, but Cecily asserts crisply, "I am not punctual myself, I know, but I do like punctuality in others, and waiting, even to be married, is quite out of the question" (E95). The play, so far from suggesting that the double life will be dispelled by marriage, suggests that it is a permanent and inescapable part of it.

As soon as the revelations of Wilde's trials were made public, it was obvious to everyone what must have been increasingly common knowledge among Wilde's friends: he was himself living a double life and had been doing so for several years. A letter to George Ives suggests the kind of Bunburying evasions that Wilde had been practicing:

"I am charmed to see you are at the Albany—I am off to the country till Monday: I have said I am going to Cambridge to see you—but I am really going to see the young Domitian, who has taken to poetry!"[1] It is possible to interpret the play as having a homosexual subtext, in which the name Ernest would become a synonym for *homosexual*. Camille Paglia has suggested that "the play's hieratic purity could best be appreciated if all the women's roles were taken by female imper- sonators."[2] The question is more than one of mere academic interest, since as soon as the play is cast and staged, the interpretation by the actors and actresses who inhabit the roles inevitably shifts the play in one of two directions. Of the Peter Hall 1982 production, Michael Billington wrote, "This is an unequivocally hetero production (I sus- pect there was nothing the least effete about the original version) in which Zoe Wanamaker's Gwendolen is no Dresden doll but a raunchy lady who, when asked by Worthing if she loves him, replies, 'Passionately,' in a voice of throaty sexiness."[3] In contrast, John Stokes, writing of the 1993 Hytner production, in which "Ernest" greeted Algy with a kiss (though this was not part of the opening night's performance), noted that the two men "romp around the sofa in a manner that cannot at this stage be purely fraternal, strengthening hopes that this might be *The Importance* our age requires."[4] Part of the strangeness of Wilde's play is that the text itself, rather than Wilde's shadow, creates the ambiguities of gender and relationship. Jack and Algy actually are brothers. Cecily, whom Algy addresses as "cousin," is a kind of niece by adoption. Jack addresses Miss Prism as "mother"; when she points him in the direction of Lady Bracknell, there is a moment when it appears that the woman who turns out to be his aunt may in fact be his mother. Cecily's socially ambiguous position as Jack's excessively pretty ward of just eighteen is commented upon by Algy. These potential monsters lurk just beneath the surface, threaten- ing any moment to emerge and create a scandal. The sense of flux is pervasive and terrifying. Against it, Wilde constructs his sculpted pat- terns of speech, gesture, and relationship, moving his characters through an elaborate series of movements until they reach a highly contrived resting place, whose icy, trivial perfection mocks the seri- ousness of the earnest Victorians and their double standards.

10

The Afterlife of Earnest

One of the distinguishing features of a major work is its reflection in other writing. Once absorbed into the collective imagination, it becomes a reference point, a means of increasing the resonance of a situation, pattern, or tone. In terms of performance, Edith Evans's seemingly definitive Lady Bracknell propelled that character into the popular imagination, so that her particular pronouncement of the terrifying question "A handbag?" has become a metaphor floating some distance from its original context. It stands for the inquisition of the young by the older generation; of children by authoritarian parents and relatives; of the socially inferior by the superior; of the unorthodox by the conventional. Lady Bracknell, like Falstaff or Alice or Huckleberry Finn, resonates outside her dramatic or theatrical setting and has become a touchstone for other characters. Reviewing Tom Stoppard's play *Arcadia,* Benedict Nightingale described Harriet Walter's performance as Lady Croom as "a Lady Bracknell with sex appeal."[1] Like the Red Queen from *Alice through the Looking Glass,* Lady Bracknell sweeps through the corridors of our minds, as well as the morning-room of Algernon's chambers or Ernest Worthing's country-house.

The first textual echo of *The Importance of Being Earnest* came in April 1895. As Kerry Powell has shown, there is a strong relationship between Wilde's play and the farce *The Foundling,* by Lestocq and Robson. *The Foundling* was presented in New York at Hoyt's Theater by the same American manager, Frohman, who was negotiating for the rights to Wilde's play. Dick Pennell wishes to marry Sophie Cotton and, like Jack Worthing, has had to admit to his prospective mother-in-law that he is parentless.

> DICK PENNELL: May I ask you what you would advise me to do? I need hardly say I would do anything in the world to secure Sophie happiness.

> MRS. COTTON: I would strongly advise you, Mr. Pennell, to try and acquire some relatives as soon as possible and to make a definite effort to produce at any rate one parent of either sex, before the season is quite over.

Powell comments that these lines complete "one of the oddest cross-fertilizations in literary history—one in which an earlier text influenced a later one, which in turn influenced a second version" of the earlier play.[2] It was also one of the fastest pieces of unacknowledged borrowing in theatrical history, presumably carried out by Frohman himself. The line stands out in sharp relief from a text whose rhythms and tone have nothing else in common with Wilde.

Shaw, as has been discussed, found himself ill at ease with Wilde's last play, after championing the earlier comedies. This did not prevent him from drawing upon it. Shaw's first "pleasant" play, *Arms and the Man,* had run from April to July 1894 at the small Avenue Theatre. *You Never Can Tell* was Shaw's attempt, as he explained it in his 1898 preface, to "comply with many requests for a play in which the much paragraphed 'brilliancy' of *Arms and the Man* should be tempered by some consideration for the requirements of managers in search for fashionable comedies for West End Theatres."[3] Shaw, then, excusing himself for the commercial pragmatism, was steeling himself to do what Wilde had accomplished so effortlessly. Shaw had, so he claimed, no difficulty in complying; far from taking "an unsympathetic view of the popular preference for fun, fashionable dresses, a little music, and even an exhibition of eating and drinking by people with an expensive air, attended by an if-possible comic waiter, I was more than willing to shew that the drama can humanize these things as easily as they, in the wrong hands, can dehumanize the drama." Shaw accused Wilde of creating heartless, dehumanized characters in *The Importance of Being Earnest*—as well as writing an old-fashioned play, one overreliant on stock situations and motifs. It amused him but had not touched him, he claimed in the *Saturday Review,* and left him with a sense of having wasted his evening. (He also contrived a subtle piece of self-promotion by mentioning, though discounting, a suggestion other critics had put forward: that *The Importance of Being Earnest* could never have been written if Shaw had not opened up entirely new paths in drama with *Arms and the Man.*)[4]

In spite of Shaw's claimed independence, *You Never Can Tell* seems to borrow a good deal of Wilde's method, in the way it both draws on and subverts the situations and motifs of farcical comedy. Like *The Foundling,* it is set in a seaside resort. Like *The Importance of Being Earnest,* it exploits the stock idea of the lost member of the family, not a baby but a father, and the accidental family reunion between the father and his three children, Gloria and the twins Dolly and Philip. The strongest echo of *The Importance of Being Earnest,* alerting one to a number of lesser parallels and correspondences, comes in Act One. Valentine is explaining to the twins why he cannot accept an invitation to lunch:

> VALENTINE: We don't bother much about dress and manners in England, because, as a nation, we don't dress well and we've no manners [a Wildean generalization, without the elegance of phrase]. But—and now will you excuse my frankness? *(They nod.)* Thank you. Well, in a seaside resort there's one thing you must have before anybody can afford to be seen going about with you; and that's a father, alive or dead. Am I to infer that you have omitted that indispensable part of your social equipment?

Whereas Wilde's play found rapid acceptance, even if the West End theater may not have fully appreciated its originality, Shaw's subversion was so complete that George Alexander confessed, after reading the typescript, that he had no more idea what Shaw meant by it than a tomcat; when the play was finally put into rehearsal, there were so many disagreements and clashes between the author and the actor-manager, Cyril Maude—to say nothing of the rest of the cast—that Shaw withdrew the play rather than compromise by rewriting. The most difficult actor was, significantly, Allan Aynesworth, Wilde's Algernon, who struggled with the part of the young dentist Valentine, and especially with the "serious" love scene with Gloria Clandon toward the end of Act Two. Michael Holroyd describes the conflict: "At one moment of exasperation Aynesworth turned on Shaw and demanded: 'Let us see you play it yourself.' Shaw sprang up on to the stage and delivered his lines. 'But that,' protested the actor, 'is comedy!' Why had no one told him they were in a comedy? It was too much."[5]

In this vital scene set on the terrace of the Marine Hotel some-where in Devon, Valentine is left alone unexpectedly with the New Woman, Gloria, with whom he has fallen in love at first sight. Gloria, as charming as Cecily but with all Gwendolen's hauteur, picks up her book and parasol:

> VALENTINE . . . *(Pretending to forget himself)*: How could that man have so beautiful a daughter!
>
> GLORIA *(taken aback for a moment; then answering him with polite but intentional contempt)*: That seems to be an attempt at what is called a pretty speech. Let me say at once, Mr. Valentine, that pretty speeches make very sickly conversation. Pray let us be friends, if we are to be friends, in a sensible and wholesome way. I have no intention of getting married; and unless you are content to accept that state of things, we had much better not cultivate each other's acquaintance.

In Act Two of *The Importance of Being Earnest*, Algernon, only recently introduced to Cecily, seizes his moment while the dogcart waits at the door:

ALGERNON: I hope, Cecily, I shall not offend you if I state quite
frankly and openly that you seem to me to be in every way the
visible personification of absolute perfection.

CECILY: I think your frankness does you great credit, Ernest. If
you will allow me, I will copy your remarks into my diary. (E61)

Shaw's scene is, in essence, the reverse of Wilde's. Algernon, in his
deceiver's role as Jack's wicked younger brother Ernest, declares his
love with extravagant eloquence, only to find it has been anticipated in
Cecily's imagination and already recorded in her diary. Valentine,
whose name proclaims his role—and, incidentally, echoes the fictional
date of Cecily and Algernon's engagement—introduces an elaborate
ploy to outwit Gloria, whose initial response is as frankly repelling as
Cecily's was unexpectedly welcoming. Cecily, the apparent innocent in
country seclusion whose education is still incomplete, remains firmly
in control; Gloria, fortified by a sophisticated life abroad and brought
up by a mother who was a veteran of the old guard of the women's
rights movement, finds herself gasping at Valentine's "We're in love
with one another" and kissed impetuously; she concludes the scene by
complaining to her mother: "Why didn't you educate me properly?"
The other reversal Shaw attempted was to overlay a complex pattern
of feelings on the scene, to challenge the heartlessness that he complained of in Wilde, as evident in the detailed commentary of his stage
directions. It is hardly surprising that the actors floundered: they found
it difficult enough to achieve the "exquisitely grave, natural, and
unconscious execution" Shaw himself had called for in performing
Wilde.[6] In spite of the slow acceptance of this particular play—Shaw
refused to go and see the first production—Wilde provided a model
for Shaw and his successors in establishing farce as a versatile and powerful dramatic form, a form capable of containing, in the right hands,
philosophical discussion, ideas about aesthetics, and social satire, and
even, as Shaw intended, feeling.

One of Shaw's criticisms of the first production of *The
Importance of Being Earnest* concerned the acting style. He accused
Alexander of spurring up for a rattling finish in the third act, of
bustling through the stage business of searching the Army Lists

instead of conducting it with subdued earnestness. Wilde's handling of the physical is, for the most part, done with precision and control. The muffins and cucumber sandwiches are devoured ferociously but elegantly; there is no hearty knockabout business, as in Pinero's *The Magistrate,* where characters eat jujubes relentlessly or slip on discarded nutshells. Shaw begins *You Never Can Tell* with the dentist Valentine extracting Dolly Clandon's tooth and ends it during a fancy-dress ball in which characters erupt into the room in dominoes and false noses and are whirled away into a final dance. Joe Orton, whose tacit acknowledgment of Wilde is evident everywhere in the style and rhythm of his language, can be seen as moving the cool amorality of *The Importance of Being Earnest* into an even more surreal world of physical comedy, drawing on the more robust tradition of French farce as well as on classical models. His last play, *What the Butler Saw* (1969), announces in its title an affinity with the world of seaside farce, of rude postcards and pier amusement machines, while the setting in a private clinic echoes the first act of *You Never Can Tell.*[7] But the verbal tone recalls, though never imitates, that of Wilde. Within seconds of the play's opening, Dr. Prentice, interviewing a prospective secretary, has asked her the crucial question, "Who was your father?" and received the reply, "I've no idea who my father was."

> PRENTICE: I'd better be frank, Miss Barclay. I can't employ you if you're in any way miraculous. It would be contrary to established practice. You did have a father?

> GERALDINE: Oh, I'm sure I did. My mother was frugal in her habits, but she'd never economize unwisely.

> PRENTICE: If you had a father why can't you produce him?

> GERALDINE: He deserted my mother. Many years ago. She was the victim of an unpleasant attack.

> PRENTICE (*shrewdly*): Was she a nun?

GERALDINE: No, she was a chambermaid at the Station Hotel.

Prentice proceeds to check Geraldine's story in a large, leather-bound volume and, like Lady Bracknell interrogating Jack, moves swiftly on:

PRENTICE: Is your mother alive? Or has she too unaccountably vanished? That is a trick question. Be careful—you could lose marks on your final scoring.

It is as though Orton is beginning where *The Importance of Being Earnest,* or a play very like it, ended. Geraldine Barclay and her twin brother, Nicholas Beckett, were, if not born and bred in a handbag at a railway cloakroom, conceived in the linen cupboard of the Station Hotel during a power-cut.[8] Changing clothes, gender, and identity during the course of the play, they each narrowly escape incest and are reunited with their unwitting parents in a recognition scene that matches the wildest fantasies of the out-of-control psychiatrist Dr. Rance. The play's epigraph is from Tourneur's *The Revenger's Tragedy:*

Surely we're all mad people, and they
Whom we think are, are not.

With this added dimension of the absurd, and Orton's Euripidean inclusion of the descent of a god in the form of the policeman Sergeant Match, in a leopard-spotted dress torn from one shoulder and streaming with blood, the play explores the subtext that lies some distance below the surface of Wilde's play: the world of Bunburying, and Ernest-in-town. In contrast to Wilde's polite solution, in which Jack assumes the mask of earnestness, Orton's final stage direction marks the full physical distance his play has traveled on this assault course through the territory of Freudian nightmare and sexual possibility. At Dr. Rance's invitation, "Let us put our clothes on and face the world," the characters "pick up their clothes and weary, bleeding, drugged and drunk, climb the rope ladder into the blazing light."

The figure of a lost, or unrecognized, son is a traditional subject, and it would be ludicrous to trace every twentieth-century English play with that theme back to Wilde. But T. S. Eliot, like Orton, was a highly conscious literary craftsman, and his contrived experiment in farce, *The Confidential Clerk* (1953), draws not just on the classical traditions of Euripides (specifically, *Ion*) and Menander but on certain locations and tones within English comedy.[9] Eliot's play revolves around three mislaid children. B. Kaghan is a foundling: "Never had any parents. Just adopted, from nowhere." He turns out, after some evidence about his christening, to be the long-lost son of Lady Elizabeth Mulhammer—"Then in order to avoid any danger of confusion," she advises him in an echo of Lady Bracknell, "you may address me as Aunt Elizabeth." Colby Simpkins, whom Sir Claude Mulhammer supposed was his son, is revealed to be the son of a disappointed musician, Herbert Guzzard, while Mrs. Guzzard, who was his mother, chose to pose as his aunt. Lucasta Angel, who has the cool poise of the orphan Cecily Cardew, is Sir Claude's illegitimate daughter, though assumed by the public to be his mistress. There are other resonances that, given the theme and the upper-class, monied atmosphere of drawing-room comedy, recall *The Importance of Being Earnest*: for example, Act Two begins in Colby's mews flat; Colby is seated at the piano. "The concluding bars of a piece of music are heard as the curtain rises." Perhaps the most striking resemblance is in the tightness and symmetry of the plot: Eliot, like Wilde, has seven main characters, including an imperious older woman used to getting her own way and an equivalent to Miss Prism in the oracular Mrs. Guzzard. But Eliot's play emphasizes the role of the father without a son, Sir Claude Mulhammer, and like a Shakespearean romance, the play concludes with the promise of the children healing the failures of their parents, an ending that has more in common with *A Woman of No Importance* than *The Importance of Being Earnest*: feeling and sentiment have worked their way back, as though Eliot was finally going back beyond Wilde to the less abrasive English tradition of eighteenth-century comedy.

Writers and audiences may glance at, or receive, echoes of Wilde in these examples. Wilde's innovations have become part of an inher-

The Afterlife of Earnest

ited tradition; in writing his play in a particular way, he subtly altered the nature of farcical comedy, and of comic writing. Noel Coward and Alan Ayckbourn are two other dramatists whose work, in tone and form, seems to have been shaped with an awareness of how Wilde wrote. Other plays from the second half of the twentieth century make more direct use of *The Importance of Being Earnest*. One is Charles Wood's *Dingo,* first performed in 1967 and published in 1969.[10] This powerful play exposes the obscenity of war; Act One is set in the Western Desert, Acts Two and Three in a prison camp. In Scene Three, with officers scraping away in a vain attempt to escape, beer crates are set on stage "for a moment of high camp drama"; the roles of Cecily, Gwendolen, and Merriman are taken by male actors impersonating blondes in bikinis and mop wigs.

MERRIMAN: Shall I lay tea as usual, miss?

CECILY: Yes, as usual.

(Merriman exits right avoiding a phallic poke from the Commandant as she goes.)

GWENDOLEN: Quite a well kept garden this, Miss Cardew.

CECILY: So glad you like it, Miss Fairfax.

The "performance" continues, an ostensible distraction for the German Commandant as the prisoners "escape" down the trap, but the savage style of the play is mocking the heroic postures of war, the officer code, and the mystique of escape lore. At the end of the sequence, the Commandant backs toward Dingo, while Gwendolen escapes down the trap; Dingo embraces the First Blonde/Cecily, who exclaims: "Let go of me. I'm a British Officer." The incongruity between the controlled elegance of the language and the physical frenzy of the action, between the connotations of tea on the country-house lawn and the squalor and degradation of war, could not be more marked. It is difficult to think of another English dramatist, with the exception of Shakespeare, who could be so confidently quoted and used for such a purpose out of context.

The most extensive dramatic response to and use of *The Importance of Being Earnest* is Tom Stoppard's *Travesties* (first produced in June 1974).[11] The play is set in Zurich during the First World War and takes place in the memory of Henry Carr, a British consular official. Other characters include Lenin, the Dadaist poet Tristan Tzara, and James Joyce; Stoppard also added a sister for Carr, Gwendolen, and a girl working in the public library, Cecily. The play revolves around the historical fact that Joyce became the business manager of the English Players, who put on a production of *The Importance of Being Earnest* in Zurich during the war. Carr really did play Algernon—"not Ernest, the other one"—in the production, and the outcome was a row, and two lawsuits, with Joyce, with claims and counterclaims about the cost of a pair of trousers and the proceeds of ticket sales. Joyce's final revenge was to find degrading roles for Carr and the consul, Henry Bennett, in the Circe episode of *Ulysses*. Stoppard, reflecting off both Joyce and Wilde, among others, in his coruscating text, allows Carr to inhabit from time to time the role of Algernon, while Bennett impersonates the tone, though not the name, of Algernon's butler, Lane. Tzara plays Jack, and Joyce, grotesquely, travesties Lady Bracknell. (Carr has assumed the surname is a Christian name and imagines Joyce to be a woman.) Stoppard uses direct quotation freely, as in (Carr) "I'm not sure that I'm much interested in your views, Bennett," or (Joyce) "Rise, sir, from that semi-recumbent posture!" He also brilliantly incorporates the idea of a fictional younger brother and the exchange, not of a baby for a three-volume novel, but of a chapter of *Ulysses* for an ill-tempered thesis of Lenin's:

JOYCE: *(thunders):* Miss Carr, where is the missing chapter???

CARR: Excuse me—did you say Bloom?

JOYCE: I did.

CARR: And is it a chapter, inordinate in length and erratic in style, remotely connected with midwifery?

JOYCE: It is a chapter which by a miracle of compression, uses the gamut of English literature from Chaucer to Carlyle to describe events taking place in a lying-in hospital in Dublin.

CARR: *(holding out his folder):* It is obviously the same work.

(Gwen and Cecily swap folders with cries of recognition. Carr and Tzara close in. A rapid but formal climax, with appropriate cries of "Cecily! Gwendolen! Henry! Tristan!" and appropriate embraces.)

Stoppard blends the text and tone of *The Importance of Being Earnest* effortlessly into his own travesty; within the fireworks, a serious three-way debate is lightly conducted about art, politics, and society, one to which the aesthetic ideas expressed by Wilde make a strong contribution. If the major protagonists are Lenin and Joyce, Wilde provides the framework and the comic tone. It is significant that Stoppard should thus link Wilde and Joyce within his fictional re-creation, transported to the center of Europe as the modern world is reshaped. Wilde's trivial play, the epitome of fiction and contrivance, the play in which the characters invent themselves, seems the most appropriate context for an encounter with Joyce, the creator of the most revolutionary fictional work of the twentieth century, *Ulysses*. Declan Kiberd, exploring the links between Wilde, Shaw, and Synge, the figure of the womanly man, and Joyce's Leopold Bloom, wrote: "What was sponsored throughout *The Importance of Being Earnest* was nothing less than the revolutionary ideal of the self-created man. . . . Jack Worthing has to androgynize himself, becoming his own father and mother, inventing his own tradition."[12] This, finally, is what Wilde has accomplished in his play. Taking the raw materials that lay to hand, he re-created a genre and invented his own tradition. *The Importance of Being Earnest* stands as a unique and individual work of art, accessible and enjoyable in itself and especially enjoyable because of its apparent and intended limitations. At the same time it functions as an act of criticism. It anticipates the surreal and the absurd, and it provides a location and a per-spective from which to view an unexpectedly broad sweep of modern literature, as well as of drama.

It has taken a hundred years for the English-speaking theater to give full recognition to Wilde's originality and to place him within the wider frame of a European perspective. In the last years of the twenti-eth century, his work, and supremely *The Importance of Being Earnest,* has acquired a new resonance, even if his characteristic sound is not the breaking string, dying away, of Chekhov but the cadences of an offstage piano or the explosion of a temperance beverage. Like Gwendolen's and Cecily's diaries, Wilde's last play is sensational and holds wonderful secrets.

Notes and References

Chapter 1

1. Vincent O'Sullivan, *Aspects of Wilde* (London: Constable, 1936), 214.

2. Frank Harris, *Oscar Wilde: His Life and Confessions* (New York: printed and published by the author, 1916; rev. ed., London: Constable, 1938), 97.

3. Rupert Hart-Davis, ed., *The Letters of Oscar Wilde* (London: Rupert Hart-Davis, 1962), 339.

4. G. B. Shaw, *Saturday Review*, 23 February 1895.

Chapter 3

1. W. H. Auden, "An Improbable Life: Review of *Letters of Oscar Wilde*," *New Yorker*, 9 March 1963.

2. *Truth*, 21 February 1895.

3. Shaw, quoted in Harris, *Oscar Wilde: His Life and Confessions.*

4. G. B. Shaw, preface to *Plays Pleasant and Unpleasant* (London: Grant Richards, 1898).

5. Max Beerbohm, *Saturday Review*, 18 January 1902. Reprinted in *Around Theatres* (London: Rupert Hart-Davis, 1953), 188–91.

6. St. John Hankin, *Fortnightly Review*, 1 May 1908: 791–802.

7. Mary McCarthy, *Sights and Spectacles* (London: Heinemann, 1959), 105.

8. Joseph W. Donohue, Jr., "The First Production of *The Importance of Being Earnest*: A Proposal for a Reconstructive Study," in *Essays on Nineteenth-Century British Theatre*, ed. Kenneth Richards and Peter Thomson (London: Methuen, 1971).

9. Kerry Powell, *Oscar Wilde and the Theatre of the 1890s* (Cambridge: Cambridge University Press, 1990), 124, 139.

10. Ian Small, *Oscar Wilde Revalued: An Essay on New Materials and Methods of Research* (Greensboro: University of North Carolina, 1993), 8. See also Joseph Donohue, "Oscar Wilde Refashioned: A Review of Recent Scholarship," in *Nineteenth-Century Theatre* 21, no. 2 (Spring 1994).

11. Katharine Worth, *Oscar Wilde* (London: Macmillan, 1983), 179.

12. David Parker, "Oscar Wilde's Great Farce," *Modern Language Quarterly* 25 (1974): 173–86.

13. Eric Bentley, *The Playwright as Thinker* (New York: Harcourt Brace, 1946), 172–77.

14. Richard Foster, "Wilde as Parodist: A Second Look at *The Importance of Being Earnest,*" *College English* 18 (October 1956): 18–23.

15. Joseph Bristow, *The Importance of Being Earnest and Related Writings* (London: Routledge, 1992), 23–24.

16. Camille Paglia, *Sexual Personae* (New Haven, Conn.: Yale University Press, 1990), 531–71.

Chapter 4

1. Manuscript letter, 9 July 1894 (Clark Library, Los Angeles).

2. *Letters,* 359; and Ian Small, *Oscar Wilde Revalued* (Greensboro, N.C.: E. L. T. Press, 1993), 65–68.

3. *Letters,* 359.

4. Powell, *Oscar Wilde and the Theatre of the 1890s,* 124–27.

5. Beerbohm, *Saturday Review,* 18 January 1902.

6. *Letters,* 368–69.

7. Hesketh Pearson, *The Life of Oscar Wilde* (London: Methuen, 1946), 254.

8. Shaw, *Saturday Review,* 12 January 1895.

9. *Letters,* 381.

10. Robert Ross, "Mr. Oscar Wilde on Mr. Oscar Wilde," *St. James's Gazette,* 18 January 1895.

11. Pearson, *The Life of Oscar Wilde,* 257.

12. 14 February is the day on which Cecily Cardew appropriately records her engagement to Ernest.

13. Ada Leverson, *Letters to the Sphinx from Oscar Wilde and Reminiscences of the Author* (London, 1930).

14. Pearson, *The Life of Oscar Wilde,* 257.

Chapter 5

1. Pearson, *The Life of Oscar Wilde,* 257.

2. John Peter, *Sunday Times,* 14 March 1993.

Chapter 6

1. Timothy d'Arch Smith, *Love in Earnest: Some Notes from the Lives and Writings of English "Uranian" Poets from 1889 to 1930* (London: Routledge and Kegan Paul, 1970).

2. See Charles B. Paul and Robert D. Pepper, "The Importance of Reading Alfred: Oscar Wilde's Debt to Alfred de Musset," *Bulletin of the New York Public Library* 75 (1971): 506–42.

3. *Letters,* 360.

4. Paglia, *Sexual Personae,* 567.

Chapter 7

1. Michael Billington, *Guardian,* 17 September 1982.

2. Pearson, *The Life of Oscar Wilde,* 257.

Chapter 8

1. Irene Vanbrugh, *To Tell My Story* (London: Hutchinson & Co., 1948), 33.

2. Beerbohm, *Saturday Review,* 18 January 1902.

3. John Gielgud, *An Actor and His Time* (London: Sidgwick and Jackson, 1979), 158.

4. *Referee,* 20 February 1895.

5. *Daily Graphic,* 15 February 1895.

6. Ross, "Mr. Oscar Wilde on Mr. Oscar Wilde," *St. James's Gazette,* 18 January 1895.

7. Beerbohm, *Saturday Review,* 18 January 1902.

8. Bentley, *The Playwright as Thinker,* 172–77.

9. Billington, *Guardian,* 17 September 1982.

10. John Stokes, *Times Literary Supplement,* 19 March 1993.

11. Irving Wardle, *Independent on Sunday,* 14 March 1993.

12. John Peter, *Sunday Times,* 14 March 1993.

Chapter 9

1. Small, *Oscar Wilde Revalued,* 58.

2. Paglia, *Sexual Personae,* 535.

3. Billington, *Guardian,* 17 September 1982.

4. Stokes, *Times Literary Supplement,* 19 March 1993.

Chapter 10

1. Benedict Nightingale, *Times,* 15 April 1993.

2. Powell, *Oscar Wilde and the Theatre of the 1890s,* 122–23.

3. Shaw, *Plays Pleasant and Unpleasant.*

4. Shaw, *Saturday Review,* 23 February 1895.

5. Michael Holroyd, *Bernard Shaw, vol. 1, 1856–1898, The Search for Love* (London: Chatto and Windus, 1988).

6. Shaw, *Saturday Review,* 23 February 1895.

7. Joe Orton, *What the Butler Saw* (London: Methuen, 1969).

8. See the more detailed discussion in Katharine J. Worth, *Revolutions in Modern English Drama* (London: G. Bell and Sons, 1975), 151–56.

9. T. S. Eliot, *The Confidential Clerk* (London: Faber and Faber, 1954).

10. Charles Wood, *Dingo* (London: Methuen, 1969).

11. Tom Stoppard, *Travesties* (London: Faber and Faber, 1975).

12. Declan Kiberd, "Bloom the Liberator," *Times Literary Supplement,* 3 January 1992, 6.

Selected Bibliography

Primary Works

The First Collected Edition of the Works of Oscar Wilde. Edited by Robert Ross. 15 vols. London: Methuen 1908; repr. 1969. A new complete and probably definitive edition of Wilde is under preparation at Oxford University Press.

Complete Works of Oscar Wilde. Introduction by Merlin Holland. Glasgow: HarperCollins, 1994. This prints a four-act version of *The Importance of Being Earnest.*

The Writings of Oscar Wilde. Edited by Isobel Murray. Oxford: Oxford University Press, 1989.

The Artist as Critic: Critical Writings of Oscar Wilde. Edited by Richard Ellmann. London: W. H. Allen, 1970.

The Complete Shorter Fiction of Oscar Wilde. Edited by Isobel Murray. Oxford: Oxford University Press, 1979.

The Importance of Being Earnest. Edited by Russell Jackson. London: Benn, 1980. This is the fullest and best edition of the play.

The Importance of Being Earnest: A Trivial Comedy for Serious People in Four Acts as Originally Written by Oscar Wilde. Edited by Sarah Augusta Dickson. 2 vols. New York: New York Public Library, Publication no. 6 of the Arents Tobacco Collection, 1956.

Lady Windermere's Fan. Edited by Ian Small. London: Benn, 1980.

The Picture of Dorian Gray. Edited by Isobel Murray. Oxford: Oxford University Press, 1974.

Two Society Comedies: A Woman of No Importance and an Ideal Husband. Edited by Ian Small and Russell Jackson. London: Benn, 1983.

Secondary Works

Bibliography, Biography, and Letters

Ellmann, Richard, *Oscar Wilde*. London: Hamish Hamilton, 1987. Far and away the best biography, incorporating a great deal of critical material, although there are several errors and a number of unsubstantiated assertions.

Fletcher, Ian, and Stokes, John. "Oscar Wilde." In *Anglo-Irish Literature: A Review of Research,* edited by Richard J. Finnernan. New York: Modern Language Association, 1976.

———. "Oscar Wilde." In *Recent Research on Anglo-Irish Writers: A Supplement to Anglo-Irish Literature: A Review of Research,* edited by Richard J. Finnernan. New York: Modern Language Association, 1983.

Hart-Davis, Rupert, ed. *The Letters of Oscar Wilde*. London: Hart-Davis, 1962. The footnotes are extensive and function almost as a biography.

———. *Selected Letters of Oscar Wilde*. Oxford: Oxford University Press, 1979.

———. *More Letters of Oscar Wilde*. London: John Murray, 1985.

Holland, Vyvyan. *Oscar Wilde: A Pictorial Biography*. London: Thames and Hudson, 1960.

———. *Son of Oscar Wilde*. London: Hart-Davis, 1954; repr. Oxford: Oxford University Press, 1988.

Hyde, H. Montgomery. *Oscar Wilde: A Biography*. New York: Farrar, Strauss and Giroux, 1975.

Mason, Stuart [Christopher Millard]. *A Bibliography of Oscar Wilde*. London: T. Werner Laurie, 1914; repr. London: Bertram Rota, 1967.

Mikhail, E. H. *Oscar Wilde: An Annotated Bibliography of Criticism*. London: Macmillan, 1978.

———, ed. *Oscar Wilde: Interviews and Recollections*. 2 vols. London: Macmillan, 1979.

Page, Norman. *An Oscar Wilde Chronology*. Boston: G. K. Hall, 1991.

Small, Ian. *Oscar Wilde Revalued: An Essay on New Materials and Methods of Research*. Greensboro: University of North Carolina, 1993. This is the most recent appraisal of current Wilde scholarship and lines of inquiry, and also prints a number of hitherto uncollected letters both from and to Wilde.

Criticism

Beckson, Karl, ed. *Oscar Wilde: The Critical Heritage*. London: Routledge and Kegan Paul, 1970. Together with the volumes edited by Ellmann and

Tydeman, this provides excellent coverage of a range of Wilde criticism, both contemporary to Wilde and more modern.

Behrendt, Patricia Flanagan. *Oscar Wilde: Eros and Aesthetics*. London: Macmillan, 1991.

Bird, Alan. *The Plays of Oscar Wilde*. London: Vision Press, 1977.

Chamberlin, J. E. *Ripe Was the Drowsy Hour*. New York: Seabury, 1977.

Dellamora, Richard. *Masculine Desire: The Sexual Politics of Victorian Aestheticism*. Chapel Hill: University of North Carolina Press, 1990.

Dollimore, Jonathan. *Sexual Dissidence: Augustine to Wilde, Freud to Foucault*. Oxford: Clarendon Press, 1991.

Ellmann, Richard, ed. *Oscar Wilde: A Collection of Critical Essays*. Englewood Cliffs, N.J.: Prentice-Hall, 1969; repr. 1986.

Ericksen, Donald H. *Oscar Wilde*. Boston: Twayne, 1977.

Gagnier, Regenia. *Idylls of the Marketplace: Oscar Wilde and the Victorian Public*. Stanford, Calif.: Stanford University Press, 1986. Gagnier places Wilde in the context of his audiences and of contemporary social institutions.

————, ed. *Critical Essays on Oscar Wilde*. New York: Twayne, 1991.

Kaplan, Joel and Sheila Stowell. *Theatre and Fashion: Oscar Wilde to the Suffragettes*. Cambridge: Cambridge University Press, 1994.

Kohl, Norbert. *Oscar Wilde: Das literarische Werk zwischen Provokation und Anpassung*. Heidelburg: Carl Winter, 1980. Translated by D. H. Wilson as *Oscar Wilde: The Work of a Conformist Rebel*. Cambridge: Cambridge University Press, 1989.

Nassaar, Christopher. *Into the Demon Universe: A Literary Exploration of Oscar Wilde*. New Haven, Conn.: Yale University Press, 1974.

Paglia, Camille. *Sexual Personae: Art and Decadence from Nefertiti to Emily Dickinson*. New Haven, Conn.: Yale University Press, 1990. A powerful reading of the unity and continuity of Western culture, with two stimulating chapters on Wilde, focusing on *The Picture of Dorian Gray* and *The Importance of Being Earnest*.

Powell, Kerry. *Oscar Wilde and the Theatre of the 1890s*. Cambridge: Cambridge University Press, 1990. Powell explores the relationship between Wilde and the late Victorian theater, providing significant details to a range of drama, much of it little known or unpublished.

Raby, Peter. *Oscar Wilde*. Cambridge: Cambridge University Press, 1988.

San Juan, Epifanio, Jr. *The Art of Oscar Wilde*. Princeton, N. J., Princeton University Press, 1967.

Shewan, Rodney. *Oscar Wilde: Art and Egotism*. London: Macmillan, 1977. A wide-ranging monograph on Wilde's work, especially perceptive on *Salomé*.

Showalter, Elaine. *Sexual Anarchy: Gender and Culture at the Fin de Siècle.* London: Bloomsbury, 1991. A wide-ranging and stimulating introduction to many aspects of the Decadents, including gender and the New Woman, with frequent references to Wilde.

Symons, Arthur. *A Study of Oscar Wilde.* London: Charles J. Sawyer, 1930. A short but valuable account of Wilde's aesthetic ideas.

Tydeman, William, ed. *Wilde, Comedies: A Selection of Critical Essays.* London: Macmillan, 1982.

Worth, Katherine. *Oscar Wilde.* London: Macmillan, 1983. The first study to concentrate on the way Wilde's plays function in performance.

Essays and Articles

Auden, W. H. "An Improbable Life." *New Yorker,* 9 March 1963, 155–71. A review of Rupert Hart-Davis's edition of Wilde's letters.

Donohue, Joseph, Jr. "The First Production of *The Importance of Being Earnest:* A Proposal for Reconstructive Study." In *Nineteenth-Century British Theatre,* edited by Kenneth Richards and Peter Thomson, 127–43. London: Methuen, 1971.

Ellmann, Richard. "Romantic Pantomime in Oscar Wilde." *Partisan Review* 30 (1963): 324–55.

Gagnier, Regenia. "Stages of Desire: Oscar Wilde's Comedies and the Consumer." *Genre* 15 (1982): 315–16.

Ganz, Arthur H. "The Divided Self in the Society Comedies of Oscar Wilde." *Modern Drama* 3 (1960): 16–23.

———. "The Meaning of *The Importance of Being Earnest.*" *Modern Drama* 6, no. 1 (1963–64): 42–52.

Glavin, John. "Deadly Earnest and Earnest Revised: Oscar Wilde's Four-Act Play." *Nineteenth-Century Studies* 1 (1987): 13–24.

Gregor, Ian. "Comedy and Oscar Wilde." *Sewanee Review* 74 (1966): 501–21.

Jordan, Robert J. "Satire and Fantasy in Wilde's *The Importance of Being Earnest.*" *Ariel* 1, no. 3 (1970): 101–9.

Kaplan, Joel H. "Ernest Worthing's London Address: A Reconsideration." *Canadian Journal of Irish Studies* 11, no. 1 (1985): 53–54.

Laity, Susan. "The Soul of Man under Victoria: *Iolanthe, The Importance of Being Earnest,* and Bourgeois Drama." In *Oscar Wilde's The Importance of Being Earnest,* edited by Harold Bloom. New York: Chelsea, 1988.

Nethercot, Arthur H. "Prunes and Miss Prism." *Modern Drama* 6 (1963–64): 112–16.

Partridge, E. B. "The Importance of Not Being Earnest." *Bucknell Review* 9, no. 2 (1960): 143–58.

Paul, Charles B., and Pepper, Robert D. "The Importance of Reading Alfred: Wilde's Debt to Alfred de Musset." *Bulletin of New York Public Library* 75 (1971): 506–42.

Poague, L. A. *"The Importance of Being Earnest:* The Texture of Wilde's Irony." *Modern Drama* 16 (1973): 251–57.

Raby, Peter. "The Making of *The Importance of Being Earnest." Times Literary Supplement,* 20 December 1991, 13.

Reinert, Otto. "The Courtship Dance in *The Importance of Being Earnest." Modern Drama* 1 (1958–59), 256–57.

Sammells, Neil. "Earning Liberties: *Travesties* and *The Importance of Being Earnest." Modern Drama* 29, no. 3 (1986): 376–87.

Spininger, Dennis J. "Profiles and Principles: The Sense of the Absurd in *The Importance of Being Earnest." Papers on Language and Literature* 12 (1976): 49–72.

Stone, Geoffrey. "Serious Bunburyism: The Logic of *The Importance of Being Earnest." Essays in Criticism* 26 (1976): 28–41.

Toliver, Harold E. "Wilde and the Importance of 'Sincere and Studied Triviality.'" *Modern Drama* 5 (1963): 389–99.

Wadleigh, Paul. "Earnest at the St. James's Theatre." *Quarterly Journal of Speech* 53 (1966): 58–62.

Ware, J. A. "Algernon's Appetite: Oscar Wilde's Hero as a Restoration Dandy." *English Literature in Transition* 13 (1970): 17–26.

Index

Index

79; significance of names in, 51–55, 62–63, 80, 90; socio-historical background, 6–7; stage directions for, 70
Inversion strategy, 64
Ionesco, Eugene, 10, 20
Ives, George, 54, 89

Jackson, Russell, 19
James, Henry: *Guy Domville*, 37; *The Turn of the Screw*, 82
Jarry, Alfred: *Ubu Roi*, 5, 10, 21
Jarvis, Martin, 59
Johnson, Lionel, 3
Jones, Henry Arthur: *The Case of Rebellious Susan*, 37; *The Triumph of the Philistines*, 5
Jonson, Ben: *Volpone,* 79
Joyce, James, 100–101

Kaplan, Joel (and Stowell): *Theatre and Fashion*, 19
Kiberd, Declan, 101

Lenin, 100–101
Lestocq, William. *See* Robson, E. M.
Leverson, Ada, 39, 40, 52, 55, 79
Lugné-Poe, A.-M., 4, 10

Malleson, Miles, 78
Marbury, Elizabeth, 8, 26
Marivaux, Pierre, 14
Marriage, 85–86, 88, 89
Maude, Cyril, 94
McCarthy, Mary, 18
Menander, 98
Midsummer Night's Dream, A, 60, 83
Millard, Evelyn, 61
Miller, Jonathan, 10

Moliere, Jean Baptiste, 15
Munro, Hugh, 47
Musset, Alfred de: *Il ne faut jurer de rien*, 53

Nesbitt, Evelyn: *The Railway Children*, 82
New Woman, 62, 94
Nightingale, Benedict, 91

Olivier, Laurence, 78
Orphans, 82
Orton, Joe: *What the Butler Saw*, 96–98

Paglia, Camille: *Sexual Personae*, 12, 22, 56, 90
Palmer, Albert, 26
Parker, David, 21
Pater, Walter, 3, 14
Peter, John, 48, 79–80
Pinero, Arthur Wing, 10, 14, 15; *Lady Bountiful*, 5; *The Magistrate*, 28, 29, 96
Pirandello, Luigi, 21
Place-names, 52–53, 54–55, 65
Powell, Kerry: *Oscar Wilde and the Theatre of the 1890s*, 19, 30, 92
Prowse, Philip, 9, 34

Queensberry, marchioness of, 53
Queensberry, marquess of, 40

Redgrave, Michael, 59, 78
Restoration comedy, 30–31
Robertson, Tom, 13
Robins, Elizabeth, 5, 6
Robson, E. M. (and Lestocq): *The Foundling*, 30, 92, 93
Ross, Robert, 17, 39, 71
Rutherford, Margaret, 78

Index

names in, 52, 53; staging of, 13, 38, 70

Importance of Being Earnest, The. See *The Importance of Being Earnest*

Lady Windermere's Fan, 5, 7, 19, 25, 31, 41, 65, 66

La Sainte Courtisane, 26

Salomé, 4, 9, 18, 22, 25

Woman of No Importance, A, 25, 31, 36, 41, 56, 65, 98;

and colonialism, 6, 7; language in, 34, 50; names in, 51, 52, 53

POETRY
Ballad of Reading Gaol, The, 4, 9

Wood, Charles: *Dingo,* 99
Worth, Katharine: *Oscar Wilde,* 18, 20
Wyndham, Charles, 6, 37

The Author

Peter Raby is head of the Drama Department at Homerton College, University of Cambridge (England). He is the author of an introductory study, *Oscar Wilde* (Cambridge University Press), and is currently editing an edition of Wilde's plays for Oxford University Press's World's Classics series. He has also written *Fair Ophelia,* a life of Harriet Smithson-Berlioz, and a literary biography of another Victorian explorer of the paradoxical, *Samuel Butler* (Hogarth Press).